The Maynard School

A Celebration of 350 years

1658–2008

Excellence in Girls' Education since 1658

First published in 2008 by
The Maynard School, Denmark Road, Exeter EX1 1SJ
www.maynard.co.uk
Registered Charity No. 1099027

British Library Cataloguing in Publication Data
A catalogue record for this book is available from
the British Library
ISBN 978-0-9560034-0-9

Designed by TRG Design, Exeter
Printed in China through Golden Cup Printing Services

Title page photo: Looking forward to Christmas 1953: End of autumn term for Upper 5A.

Contents

List of Illustrations

Acknowledgements

AS WITH ANY VOLUME OF THIS NATURE, heartfelt thanks are due to many people, without whom it would never have seen the light of day: all the contributors named within the text, who so kindly took time out to write about their Maynard memories or accounts of the School; those long gone but who left a legacy of great treasures in our archive in the form of photographs, press cuttings and magazine reports (I have come to know them just as well as any living Maynardians), and the many others who have provided additional material and precious nuggets of information or checked the text as it took shape, in particular: Lois Beaton (Lane), Veronica Clarke, Fiona Dawrant, Mary Ellis, Jean Hall, Margaret Ham, Lyn Hope, Sally Hoult, Tom Hughes-Parry, Mary Hyde, Freda Jackson, Bridget Kirby, Jane Meredith, Felicity Murdin, Daphne West, Kevin White and Sylvia Wickenden.

Extra-special thanks must go to Julie Dawick who, thinking she had retired from teaching English and History in 2007, found she was spending just as much time in School trawling through piles of old documents (not to mention all the hours in the Devon Record Office), having rashly offered to 'help' with both the archive and this book! Julie's input has been invaluable — both her prodigious research and as a wonderfully positive voice of calm and reason when deadlines seemed insurmountable. Thank you Julie!

Doris Bradbeer, a Maynard School Governor from 1948 to 1986, undoubtedly had a point when she wrote in 1974: 'If a well-meaning friend suggested that you might profitably occupy your time by writing a factual account of a school, or a person, or a place of interest, I should strongly advise you to think very carefully before making up your mind—and then decide to fill up your leisure time in some other way!'

However, this book is not intended to take the place of Miss Bradbeer's superbly detailed and researched 1972 book *Joyful Schooldays* which has been an invaluable resource for this modest publication. It is more a cornucopia of memories, impressions, events and images reflecting aspects of daily life in the school, how it has changed throughout the centuries and how it has fitted into the social scene of the time. Essentially, I hope this book will provide tiny 'windows' through which the reader can glimpse the lives of Maynardians and their (mostly!) much-loved school down the ages, and the times in which they lived, and also give an insight into some of the personalities and events that have shaped the Maynard into the unique and very special School it is today.

Donna Sharp
Archivist 2004–2008

Schooling for Girls

Julie Dawick
(History and English teacher, 1994–2007)

FOUNDED IN THE MID-17TH CENTURY, the Maynard School is the third oldest girls' school in the country, after Bristol Red Maids' (1634), and New Hall in Chelmsford (1642). For centuries, the focus of girls' education outside their own homes had been basic literacy and needlecraft skills, either in convent schools or upper-class private households. The idea of extending this to girls from more lowly backgrounds took the form of charitable foundations, such as that which set up the Maynard School, for girls who would not otherwise expect to receive a formal education.

From the 17th century onwards, girls from middle- and upper-class families were often sent away to school to acquire 'accomplishments', such as music, drawing, dancing and modern languages. But in the 19th century, some pioneering women educationalists took girls' education onto a more ambitious level, including Science and Classics, rather than just literacy and accomplishments. This change was spearheaded by the London foundations of Queen's College (1848), and Bedford College (1849), providing lectures to improve the education of teenagers and young women who intended to begin a teaching career, which at that time was the only socially acceptable way for educated women to earn a living. Two of the students from Queen's went on to found girls' schools: Frances Mary Buss at the North London Collegiate School in 1850, and Dorothea Beale at Cheltenham in 1858. By 1864 there were 20 endowed schools for girls compared to 820 boys' schools, but from the 1870s onwards, the foundation of girls' schools really gathered momentum, and women's colleges were opened at London, Oxford and Cambridge Universities, although this was in the face of some social resistance, with Oxbridge degrees not being formally awarded to women for decades. In the early 20th century, this situation led to an unusual episode when Trinity College, Dublin, introduced the award of full degrees to women who had also successfully completed university courses at Oxford or Cambridge. These *ad eundem* (same status) degrees were attractive to women Oxbridge 'graduates', because although London and Durham awarded full degrees to their women students, Oxford withheld these until 1920, and Cambridge until 1947, and their students felt disadvantaged when competing for professional posts as academics and schoolteachers. From 1904 to 1907, over 700 women who had studied at Oxford and Cambridge travelled to Dublin and paid between £10 and £16 to be officially awarded degrees. These 'steamboat ladies', as they were called, included Emily Penrose, principal of Somerville, Oxford; Margaret Tuke, principal of Bedford College, London; Sara Burstall, Head of Manchester Girls' High School; and the Headmistress and two other members of the staff at Exeter Girls' High School (The Maynard School). The school magazine recorded that, 'The year 1905 has been noteworthy by reason of the very large number of women students of Oxford and Cambridge who have availed themselves of the opportunity given them by Trinity College, Dublin, of taking their *ad eundem* BA and MA Degrees. Miss Purdie, Miss Shearson and Miss Carters have already journeyed to Dublin this year for that purpose, and it seems not unlikely that other members of staff may soon proceed to MA or even possibly DLitt'. Trinity College ended the *ad eundem* arrangement in 1907 because Irish women students were beginning to transfer their studies to the Oxbridge colleges where the residential facilities were better, but the money raised from the 'sale' of their degrees was put towards setting up residences for their home-grown female students.

Miss Purdie was Head of the Maynard School from 1902 to 1908, but she might have been concerned at the sentiments expressed by one of the guest speakers at Speech Day in 1925. Principal Murray, from Exeter University, emphasised that girls should have an adequate training in the Domestic Arts. It was wrong for girls to take Higher Education and 'take what boys had'. He suggested that the recent trend towards equality was not appropriate. This attitude is taking a long time to change, and even as recently as 20 years ago, a member of the local landed gentry, who shall be nameless, was heard to complain in all seriousness that despite sending his son to Winchester in time-honoured family tradition, the son had been unable to get into Oxford as expected, because all the places were taken up (i.e. wasted) by girls.

So, in terms of absolute equality, is there still some work to be done?

From small beginnings…

The Foundation of the School

THE MAYNARD FAMILY IN DEVON originated from Axminster, and a 14th-century John Maynard of that town fought with The Black Prince in the Hundred Years' War. By the 16th century, his direct descendants, a succession of John or Nicholas Maynards, were living at Sherford near Kingsbridge. Of the four sons of John Maynard of Sherford in the late 16th century, the eldest, Nicholas, inherited the paternal estate, while the fourth son, Alexander, settled at Tavistock, and married Honora Arscott of Tetcott, near Holsworthy. Of their four sons, John (later Sir John Maynard), was the only survivor into adulthood. Sir John's career progressed from a steady beginning as a lawyer at the Middle Temple, to MP for Totnes in the 1640s, and MP for Plymouth in 1689, the year before his death. He played a prominent role in the political upheavals of the 17th century, being involved in the impeachments of the King's advisers, the Earl of Strafford and Archbishop Laud. Although he was briefly imprisoned by Cromwell for his opposition on some constitutional points, he managed to keep his political career on track, becoming Sergeant-at-Law for the new republican government, and was one of the committee engineering the constitutional transition to the restored monarchy in 1660. He amassed a very large fortune and in 1656 bought an estate at Gunnersbury, near Ealing in London. In 1663 he commissioned John Webb, pupil and son-in-law of Inigo Jones, to rebuild the manor house in the grand Palladian style. After John's death on 9th October 1690 his body lay in state at Gunnersbury House for 16 days after which he was buried 'with great pomp' at nearby Ealing Church.

Sir John Maynard 1602–1690
(National Portrait Gallery, artist unknown)

Gunnersbury House, as designed and built for Sir John Maynard by John Webb. It was demolished and rebuilt as two properties in 1801

John Maynard had one son, Joseph, and four daughters, Elizabeth, Honora, Johanna and Martha, all by Elizabeth Henley, his first wife. After Elizabeth's death in 1654/55 he married Jane Selhurst and after Jane's death in 1668 he married Margaret Prujean, the widow of Sir Francis Prujean, president of the Royal College of Physicians. His fourth and last wife was Mary Vermuyden, widow of Sir Charles Vermuyden. She inherited Gunnersbury House and survived John by 31 years, eventually marrying Henry Howard, 5th Earl of Suffolk. There is an intriguing entry in the 1693 Minute Book of the Blue Maids' School referring to £4 being paid 'towards the carriage of Elizabeth Kent (a mayd of this house) to London, at ye instance and desire of my Lady Maynard.' Was this Mary, Sir John's widow, taking in one of the early 'Maynard' girls as a servant at Gunnersbury?

Except for possibly his youngest daughter, all John Maynard's children pre-deceased him so he left his estate in trust to his grandchildren. The terms of his will were so obscure that it had to be settled by litigation and a private Act of Parliament. Both Johanna and one of his granddaughters, Elizabeth, made good matches into, respectively, the Leghs of Adlington Hall in Cheshire and the Hobart family of Blickling Hall in Norfolk. There are portraits of Sir John at both places; also in the National Gallery, at Exeter College, Oxford, where he resided in 1621, and at Middle Temple. Johanna and Thomas Legh had five children and, in a strange twist, centuries later an Old Maynardian's daughter also married the owner of Adlington Hall. In the 1955–56 *Maynard Magazine* Evangeline France-Hayhurst (Chaworth-Musters) recounts how, on a visit to Adlington for the christening of her grandson, she suddenly found herself staring up at the Maynard School Crest. 'In considerable astonishment I asked my son-in-law what my School hat badge was doing on his ceiling.'

The story of the Maynard School itself begins with a very wealthy Devon squire, Elize Hele. He was childless, and being unimpressed with his nephew, he left his fortune after his death in 1635 to be allocated by four trustees for 'godly and pious uses'. This was a very wide brief, and over the next 20 years, an Oxford lectureship, a library, prison improvements, and a good few Devon schools benefited from the trustees' choices. By the 1650s, only two trustees were still living and carrying out their duties – John Maynard, related to Hele's wife, Alice, and Elize Stert, a family friend. Their work was greatly hampered by the upheavals of the civil war and Sir John's duties as Sergeant-at-Law to the new republican government, but they made a decision in 1656 to set up a charitable school for poor girls in Exeter as part of the 'godly and pious uses' of Elize Hele's legacy. It should have more correctly been called 'Maynard and Stert's Girls' School Foundation of

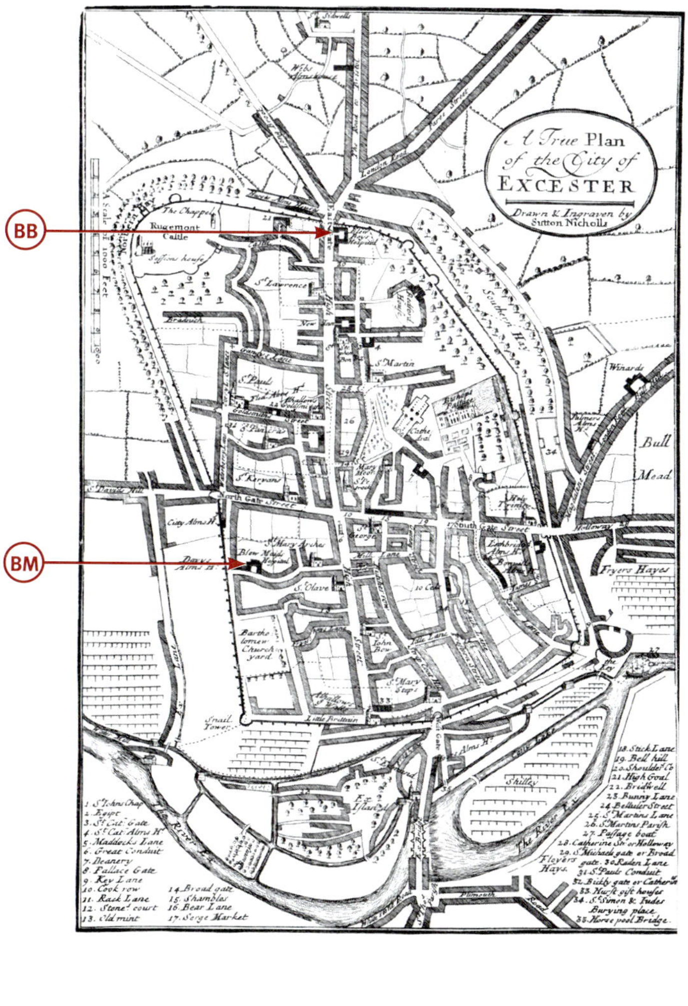

Sutton Nicholls' Map showing location of 'Blew Maids Hospital' (BM), The Great House in Mary Arches Street, and 'Blew Boys Hospital' (BB) at what is now the High Street/Princesshay junction.

The School Motto

(as published in the school magazine 1960–61)

Manus Justa Nardus,
We know the motto well;
But what it means, or what it meant,
No dictionary can tell.

Manus, we see plainly,
Is Latin for a hand.
It's fourth declension nominative,
And feminine in clan.

That explains the *Justa*
Agreeing, as it must,
A first declension adjective
To be translated 'just'.

Nardus, on the other hand,
Is really quite absurd.
Our Latin books small aid can give
To help us find the word.

'Nardus' says the dictionary:
'A thick perennial herb'.
But why a noun in such a place?
We surely need a verb!

Then we find that *nardus*
Is blessed with fragrant scent.
Originally from India,
It provides a soft unguent.

Manus Justa Nardus,
As bad as an unseen!
'A just hand (is) a healing balm'
It's really thought to mean.

The truthful explanation
For such obscurity
Is – the motto sounds like 'Maynard'.
This you cannot fail to see.

Why worry if the *'nardus'*
Appears a little strange?
At least the *'manus justa'*
Is well within our range.

And so to Maynard scholars,
And to any others too,
Let's carry hands of justice forth
Until our life is through!

Celia Smith, LVI Armourer

Hele's Charitable Endowment', but Maynard and Stert referred to it as 'Hele's Hospital', and in any case, it quickly became popularly known as the 'Blue Maids' Hospital' because of the uniform worn by the pupils.

The First Two Hundred Years

The title 'hospital' referred to any institution involving care of, or charitable benefactions to, society's poor in days when social care was in not in any way a responsibility of the state. The first Exeter girls to benefit from Hele's charity may have shared the East Gate premises of The Blue Boys at St John's Hospital, who had also benefited greatly from Hele's Trust money. But in 1662, Maynard and Stert purchased the Great House in Mary Arches Street for £600 as a separate school for the Blue Maids, and they passed responsibility over to the City Council. The house was already about 200 years old, and shown on old maps with medieval fortifications of turrets and castellations, but for the next 200 years it housed a fluctuating number of poor girls and their schoolmistress. The new trustees, Exeter City Council, mismanaged the School's endowment income very badly, and there was often only a handful of girls.

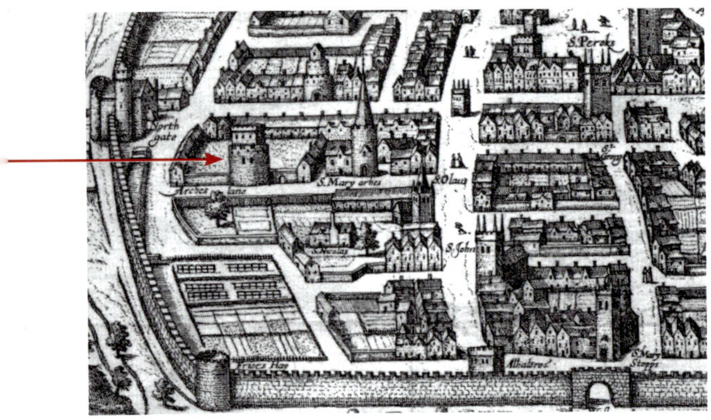

Section of earlier 1618 map depicting the castellated Great House in Mary Arches Street.

The foundation document of 1656 allowed for £10 a year to be spent on each Blue Maid, for as many girls as the endowment money 'would reach unto', and the City Council paid £20 annual stipend for a schoolmistress, although they seemed to have 'reclaimed' this money by only allowing £6 per girl. Three of the early minute books of the Hospital survive and give us the names of some personalities who filled the role of Mistress. It seems to have been a family affair, with the post often passing from mother to daughter (see page 97). The responsibilities included making sure that the girls were adequately provided with clothes and bed linen, and schooling the girls in basic literacy and needlework skills. This responsibility seems to have been rather erratically carried out between 1692 and 1707, when Mrs Wilmott Martin was the Mistress. At one point she took up residence off site with a Mr Henry Cudmore and in 1697 the minute books ordered that 'Notice be given to Mr Henry Cudmore that the Governess of the Hospitall will quitt his house at Midsomer next where the Governess now resides.' Perhaps she was moonlighting as a housekeeper to boost her income? In 1703, she was given precise instructions on how to oversee the girls' education. It was 'ordered that the children of this house be from henceforward Two days at Spinning, Two days at Knitting, and Two days at Plain Worke.' It was possibly because of her lax supervision that one of the girls, Christian Heard, was able to steal money from the servant of the Hospital. Christian was ordered to be expelled, unless her father could find an apprenticeship for her, and he was apparently successful, as the next month she was 'bound out to James Commins, pipemaker.' The girls were only provided for at the School until they were 14, when they returned home to their parents, or left for an apprenticeship. Some were sent home early because they were ill – Grace Smart in 1678 'by reason of a malady called the King's Evil,' and Joan Rea in 1709 sent to her mother 'having the King's Evil and Bad Eys.' Christian Heard was not the only miscreant, as Hannah Ceely, who was 'bound apprentice to Josiah Lee, baker, on 14th December, was refused by him on 21st December on account of her immorality.' The hospital refused to take her back. In the 1730s, the Mistress was Mrs Margaret Mayne, and the overseer from the City Council had to remind her of the duty to educate the girls by specifying that the children be 'taught to read twice every day with an hour in the forenoon and an hour in the evenings.' The minute books don't report on the effectiveness of this double 'Literacy Hour'.

In the 1680s, the girls shared the building with wounded soldiers from William of Orange's successful invasion against James II, and the City Council wrote many subsequent letters to the Treasury, trying to get repaid for the medical care given to the soldiers. In the early 1800s some rooms in the Great House were rented out to another charitable school, Wootton's Charity School – for boys – and in both cases, the schoolmistress would have earned her stipend trying to shield the girls from the possible bad language and boisterous behaviour of these other residents.

The financial state of the School was so bad by the 1860s that the government's Charity Commission recommended the closure of the School in 1862. The endowment money was reabsorbed by the St John's Hospital

Trust, and used to finance poor girls through the Episcopal, National and Central Schools in the City. The Great House was sold and soon demolished, and Maynard and Stert's foundation went through a period of limbo.

The 'New' Maynard School

In an effort to fulfil the original benefaction of 'a school for poor girls', money was reallocated from the St John's Hospital Trust for the foundation of the Maynard School for Girls in 1877, at the time more commonly known as Exeter High School for Girls (this can still be seen on the Denmark Road entrance pillars if you look closely), the official change of name not taking place until 1911, as recorded in the School magazine: 'Another change is in the name of the School, that we may not forget our revered founder. In the future our School will be known as The Maynard School.'

But in 1877, until suitable premises could be bought or built, the School was accommodated in the Council-owned Larkbeare House near St Leonard's Church. This was also used periodically to house the Assize judges, and on those occasions, the girls' School was forced to rent other premises. In 1878, a suitable site was purchased for a purpose-built school between Denmark Road and Spicer Road, a plot that had just been rejected by the boys' Grammar School (later Exeter School), and the first School buildings were completed in 1882.

The new School could accommodate up to 150 pupils, and the premises were enhanced by the opening of the School Hall just over a year later in 1883, featuring a splendid stained glass window depicting, for inspiration, the figures of Chaucer, Spenser, Milton, Bacon and Shakespeare. The Hall was further adorned after the death of the School's second Head, Caroline Turner, when Harry Hems, a famous local craftsman and businessman with a handsome workshop and house in Longbrook Street, added oak panelling under the stained glass window, inscribed in memory of Miss Turner with her favourite motto: 'The very true beginning of wisdom is the desire of discipline'.

Early records

For such a long-established School, there is not a wealth of early records, as Miss Purdie, the School's third Head, found when she set up the Old Girls' Society on her arrival in 1902. Her report in the first School magazine of that year said, 'On hunting up School registers to get a complete list of names, it was found that no record had been preserved at School farther back than 1891' (when the School's second Head, Caroline Turner, took over from Miss Hall).

This situation was made worse by the loss of all the School records that were in the Clerk's Office at Summerlands boarding house, which was completely destroyed in the Exeter Blitz raid of 1942. So early impressions of the School are mainly gleaned from items in the annual School magazine, set up and first published by the energetic Miss Purdie in 1902, and which have survived as an almost complete set.

Expansion of the School

The School was established on its new site in 1882 with 40 pupils in the first term, and if this seems to be quite a modest start, it was larger than the small beginnings of the School in Larkbeare five years earlier. When the first Headmistress, Nora Hall (1877–1891), returned to the School in 1902 to be guest speaker at the first meeting of the revived Old Girls' Society, she reported that the School had opened at Larkbeare in 1877 with nine girls and three mistresses. The new School buildings of 1882 could accommodate 150 pupils, and this number was quickly reached and more or less maintained until after the First World War, when numbers increased rapidly to 243 in 1919, and 300 in 1935. Successive Heads made steady efforts on a limited budget to improve facilities.

Miss Nora Hall, Headmistress 1877–1891, the first Head in the 'new' building.

Form sizes fluctuated greatly. In 1904, the Upper 4 was reduced to 10 (from 16) because so many girls left over the course of the year. On other occasions, epidemic illnesses decimated form numbers. In 1909, the Upper 4 wrote 'there are 13 girls in our form, but unfortunately during the summer, four of us had to stay away on account of measles.' The situation was worse in Form 2 when 11 out of 18 were absent the whole summer term because of the measles scare. Another measles outbreak in 1913 caused similar disruption. The Upper 5 wrote in the School magazine, 'In the spring term the

Miss Purdie, Headmistress 1901–1908, in her sitting room.

measles unfortunately visited us, and only four of us were left out of fifteen. It was quite exciting having lessons by ourselves, and if the truth be known, we rather enjoyed it. Of course, we were extremely sorry for the absentees, and perhaps they were sorry for us'. Not only measles, but the other dangerous disease of diphtheria struck in 1914. There were 17 girls that year in Lower 5, but 'there were only two left in the middle of the [summer] term when diphtheria broke out, the rest of us all having been scared away'.

In 1904, lighting for the School was improved by Miss Purdie, when the basic open-flame gas burners were replaced by the new incandescent gas mantles – Miss Purdie reporting that 'the School ought not to be behindhand in such an elementary necessity as satisfactory illumination'. This was again updated in 1924 with the installation of electric lighting throughout the School.

Heating was provided by open fires in the classrooms, and hot water 'coils' in the corridors. Keeping the open fires 'primed' during lesson times was obviously too inconvenient, and hot water radiators fired by a solid fuel boiler were extended from the corridors into the classrooms in 1905. This was much appreciated by Maynardians of the time: 'The comfort of the School is much enhanced this winter by the extension of the hot water apparatus to the Classrooms, and by additions to the coils in the Hall and Corridors. A very snug and cosy feeling now prevails in the building whatever the weather.' However, it seems that the fires had to be reinstated during the harsh winter of 1917. A Form 2 pupil wrote 'We had to have a fire this winter for the hot water pipes would not work.' The new solid fuel boiler system had a dedicated caretaker whose special responsibility it was to stoke the boilers. Freda Jackson remembers that when she was in Upper 4, on one cold day early in February 1953, they were all kept waiting outside School and eventually directed into the Hall where they were told to go back home as the boiler had burst during the night. 'Returning to School a few days later we found portable heaters in the classrooms. These were moved around the room at intervals to share out the warmth. Later in the term I remember doing School exams wearing gloves, and removing them reluctantly to draw accurate angles in a Maths exam.' The Library, however, retained a gas fire long after all others were abandoned because the heating was so inadequate at that distance from the boilers. In 1963 the solid fuel system was replaced by an oil-fired system at a cost of £3,500. This was put under immediate strain when the severe winter of 1963 froze all the heating pipes. The School was one of the few in Exeter to open at the start of the January 1964 term after the caretaking team's strenuous efforts to thaw out the pipes.

In 1935, Speech Day, as it was then known, was moved away from the School premises for the first time to the Barnfield Theatre when larger numbers of parents and visitors needed to be accommodated because the one-time Dean of Exeter, Dr Matthews, was coming back to present the prizes in his new role as Dean of St Paul's Cathedral. Dr Matthews also opened the Purdie Memorial Library in 1938, and he visited again in 1958 to celebrate the tercentenary of the School, when a special speech day was held in the Civic Hall and a service in the Cathedral, at which the Staff had to wear hats. By 1969 it had moved to the Great Hall at Exeter University, a development that a member of that year's Lower Sixth had much to say about: 'This year's Speech Day, held again in the University Great Hall, followed the traditional pattern, but those who believe that constant change is necessary to prevent stagnation were satisfied by a different seating arrangement, for this year Maynardians were allowed to sit with their guests. This allayed what must be the usual feelings of the parents, that they are herded together and segregated from their offspring. Whether we appreciated the change so much is more doubtful, since most of the School had to work during the morning instead of spending it trapesing [sic] to and from the Great Hall! … we were far more interested by Miss Bradley's announcement that a new £24,000 Sixth Form block is to be built within the grounds, freeing the present Sixth Form rooms, both small and inconvenient, for general use. A new Building Appeal is to be launched for this purpose, and it seems as though we shall be holding Grandes Fêtes for years to come.' The following year Speech Day became an evening event for the first time and in 1971 another, much welcomed, adjustment was made: 'Once again Speech Day took place in the evening … The one major difference was the position of the orchestra which, this year, was on the platform behind our guests. We made this arrangement because some of the visitors in the gallery had been unable to see the orchestra in previous years. The innovation was a great success …' In 1972

Speech Day became Prize Giving and, apart from in 1985 when it was held in the newly-opened Bradley Hall, it has been held at the University Great Hall, following much the same format, ever since.

Meal provision was a notable feature of the School's facilities from 1900 onwards, and many of the early 20th-century School inspection reports noted favourably the hot dinners provided by the School's own kitchens. In 1925, the famous 'bun ticket' system was started to provide milk, buns or doughnuts at break and lunchtimes. In 1946, during Miss Ryan's headship, the new Family Allowance Act meant that the School had to supply many more School dinners, with numbers up from 140 to 300. After six years of argument with the Ministry of Works, who wanted a pre-fabricated building, a new dining centre built of traditional materials was constructed for £10,500. It opened in July 1954 and served 367 meals on the first day.

Bun tickets, one of the most abiding Maynardian memories! Right up until the early 1970s they were sold in books, with sufficient tickets for one term, and enabled the holder to choose from, usually, a cream bun, a Chelsea bun or a doughnut.

Miss Bradley's arrival in 1962 brought changes to the School buildings, including the small adjustment of removing a slice of the staging in the Hall to allow a fire escape to a new side door, and on a much larger scale, building a new Sixth Form block alongside the gym (built in 1957), because numbers in the Sixth Form had doubled between 1963 and 1968. Work was completed in 1970 at a cost of £28,000, and named after Miss Ryan who had steered the School through so much, not least the difficult war years. A collection from the pupils paid for a commemorative plaque and the re-planting of the Rose Garden. Extra space in main school, produced by Art and Domestic Science relocating to Tregear when boarding ceased there, allowed for an additional form room, a library extension and an extra staff common room and Chemistry laboratory.

A sign of the changing times was the setting up of the School Council in 1969. Representatives from each form and the staff started to meet once a term to discuss different suggestions, an early decision resulting in the installation of an automatic hot drinks machine in the grounds! In the 1974 school magazine one Sixth Former reflected more seriously on how Maynard life had changed, '… one appreciates the changes which have developed gradually over the years – changes which have resulted in a situation of pleasant freedom for the Sixth Form. Now with our common room coffee-bar run by volunteers, afternoons devoted to recreation of our own choice and the opportunity to wear our own clothes, the slow climb up through the School seems to have been rewarded. Moreover, with School Council well established, the girls in the Main School now have a say in matters which affect them.' By 1969 there was also a question mark over the House System: 'During the year there has been much discussion about the House System. Some people felt that it no longer served a useful purpose, and others, that more would be achieved if there were more Houses containing fewer people. However, it was finally agreed that the four Houses would remain intact, and further effort would be exerted to encourage the group spirit and co-operation for which they were intended.' Although the Houses were saved it is probably true that they were no longer regarded as quite so important, which was further confirmed by House Reports ceasing to appear in the school magazine after 1990.

Before her retirement in 1979, Miss Bradley had to guide the School through the great changes brought about by the ending of Direct Grant status in 1975. This had been in place since 1922, and the change would alter the whole balance of School funding. In response to this, the School decided to become fully independent. The free places were phased out over a seven year period and replaced in 1980 by the Assisted Places Scheme. This scheme offered financial help towards independent school fees for bright children from families of modest means. However, the Assisted Places scheme in its turn was also phased out in 2001, but some assistance with fees was still continued with help from the Governors.

By the time of Miss Murdin's arrival in 1980 numbers had increased to such an extent that some hard decisions had to be taken. Miss Murdin explained in her 1981 Prize Giving Report: 'What we very much wish to do is to initiate three parallel forms from Lower Fourth upwards, starting next September when this year's Upper Thirds move forward. Each group will have a maximum size of 24, a very much more favourable number than the present 30 for form subjects, and for effective pastoral care. We shall be able to use our classrooms in Main School more flexibly: at present some rooms are bursting at the seams, making it impossible for staff to get round to individual pupils at their desks.' In order to find the necessary space to facilitate this change it had been decided to phase out Kindergarten and Transition. This was a difficult decision not taken lightly but made easier by the pending retirement of Miss Sparks, the Head of Junior School. This would mark the end of an era in many ways and both Miss Sparks and the Junior School staff had given their backing to the plan. Miss Murdin went on to say: 'The use of the Traceyville building by older girls, probably the 10-year-olds, will draw the whole School more closely together, and from this must derive much general educational benefit to Junior and Main School alike, quite apart from ensuring the optimum use of facilities. A three-form pattern will involve a certain amount of extra staffing, but the cost of this and any building scheme can to a large extent be covered by an increased intake.'

The management of the School was now having to take more account of modern competition, and the first Open Evening was held in 1989, helping to raise the profile of the School. The second one was in 1991, and has since been an annual, and now biannual, event.

The Maynard Parents' Association held its first meeting in 1981, and quickly established an important support role in the life of the School. The first event was a social one, recorded in the School magazine as 'a wine and cheese party'.

The first male member of staff arrived in 1972 – Ken Swift, who taught Physics (later Head of Physics and, after his retirement, Archivist). This was a significant development for the School – and in one instance for members of staff personally. In 1990 the Maynard celebrated its first (and only, so far) school wedding: Nick Horton, Director of Music, and Alison Lindsay, Maths teacher, were married in Exeter Cathedral on 6th August. Members of both the Choral Society and the Senior School Choir sang; and Upper 3N, Miss Lindsay's form, greeted them with a floral arch when they came out by the West Door. Mr and Mrs Horton are still on the staff, and have a 15-year-old son, Tom.

In 1982, a building appeal was launched for a new sports hall, to be named Bradley Hall after the recently-retired Head. In 1985, the School celebrated its completion, and the welcome availability of a very large space, by holding Prize Giving on-site for the first time since 1935, with platforming borrowed from Mount St Mary's School. In her Headmistress's report for the year, Miss Murdin gave an amusing insight into the realities of headship: 'A Headmistress of my acquaintance has described her job as comparable to driving a bus-full of backseat drivers in the dark down an unknown road in the pouring rain. Well, perhaps there are times when one wonders whatever's coming next, or even wishes that a passenger or two would get off, but I feel that our drive through 1985 couldn't have been pleasanter. We have arrived at a splendid stopping-point in this celebration of Bradley Hall tonight and we look forward to getting into gear for 1986.'

'Topping out' of Pring, 1991. L-R George Clark (Mayor), Kate Johnson (Head Girl), Miss Murdin, Ken Rowe (Maynardian Old Boy), Terry Knapp (Builder). (Photo courtesy Exeter Express & Echo.)

In July 1990 the Governors agreed unanimously to go ahead with their plans to provide a new building for teaching Physics, Chemistry, Biology, Mathematics and Computer Studies. This was considered at the time to be the largest and most important development to have taken place since the School was built. The 1954 dining centre was demolished to provide enough space on a crowded site and, in 1991 the new Pring building (named after Herman Pring, Chairman of the Governors 1959–73) was completed.

The School was always keen to maintain a lead in educational developments, and as early as 1968, Sixth Form pupils went to the Technical College for a Computer Appreciation and Programming course as part of the General Studies programme. In 1983, a computer room was set up, with Computer Studies introduced into the Sixth Form syllabus, and in 1995 the Maynard was the first school in Devon (and one of the first in the country) to get full internet connectivity.

The more recent development of Computer Studies (now called ICT) within the School has resulted in the fitting out of the Wolfson Room (so named to mark the significant grant for the project from the Wolfson Foundation) near the School library as a second, dedicated ICT room, as well as the development of network services in the former 'stoke hole' where the coal-fired boiler was once situated – a complete transformation from outdated heating technology to ultra-modern communications technology.

The School Songs

The official School Song first appeared in 1920, the same year that the House system was introduced. It was composed jointly by Miss Lily Parsons and Miss Mary Alcock and was received enthusiastically: 'Our thanks are due to Miss Parsons for writing such a jolly, inspiring school song, and to Miss Alcock for composing such a delightful tune. It is always the first song we strike up when charabancing [sic] home ...'

When the match is lost or won,
And we are homeward wending,
When the long term's work is done
With mirth to greet its ending;
When met again in after days
We set the hall a-ringing
With laughter bred of memories,
Then is the time for singing:
Filiae Devonienses,
Portemus, Exonienses,
Manus justas, velut enses,
Honoris causa Maynardi!

At School we learn a crowd of things
Both dull and interesting,
The names and dates of English Kings,
And sums about investing;
To tell no tales; whate'er betide
Keep faith; be prompt in giving;
Play not for self, but for the side –
And ours the life worth living!
Filiae Devonienses, ...

Good indeed our heritage
From rougher years of striving,
When pious gentlemen and sage
Were for our weal contriving;
And Blue Maids still, our duty calls
Clear as a trumpet's pealing,
Favourites of Fortune or her thrall,
Keep we the hand right dealing!
Filiae Devonienses, ...

Many years later a second 'school song' developed:

There's something about the Maynard,
There's something about the Maynard,
There's something about the Maynard,
that is fine, fine, fine.

It may be the noble founder,
It may be the great Headmistress,
It may be the youngest junior
in the line, line, line.

There's something about their bearing,
There's something in what they're wearing,
There's something about their bright eyes
all a-shine, shine, shine.

Oh, the young Maynardian
Makes me say just once again:
There's something about the Maynard
that is fine, fine, fine.

Sung to the tune of *There's Something About a Soldier,* written in the 1930s, no-one is quite sure how this came about but, according to a letter from Miss Anderson to Miss Murdin in 1982: '... it was used in a House production 'Goldy Smith & the 3Rs' and various other extravaganza before it caught on as a School song.'

Whatever the truth of the matter, both songs are sung with great gusto; the latter as everyone marches out, at every end-of-term assembly including the Leavers' Assembly in the summer.

Form rooms

2008: English teacher, Mrs Viv Martin, with the 1904 Maynard crocodile that she rescued.

THERE WERE ORIGINALLY NO NUMBERS for the classrooms, and they were distinguished by the paintings hung on the walls. Each room specialised in a particular 'school' of art, for example, the Tuscan Room, the Dutch Room, and the Spanish Room. The pictures were provided by the Kyrle Society, started within the school in 1902 or 1903 to raise money for beautifying the school's surroundings. This national society had been founded in 1876 to better the life of working people by enhancing their surroundings by, for example, improving rooms and gardens of hospitals, missions and schools, developing parks and encouraging house decoration and flower growing. It was one of the first civic amenity bodies and was named after the famous philanthropist John Kyrle of Gloucestershire (also known as the Man of Ross), who spent his energies in benevolent acts in his neighbourhood. The Maynard School's Kyrle Society paid for paintings, oak panelling and curtains for the Hall; also clocks, plants and inkwells.

As well as paintings, girls were encouraged to improve the rooms with flowers and objects of interest. There was usually a flower monitor, and one of the younger classes even started a little museum: (Upper 1 in 1904) 'We thought we would start a museum. Miss Purdie gave us … two snakes which are poisonous. We have some nice fossils and some sea urchins. One girl brought some foreign money. Then somebody gave a beautiful crocodile with a lovely long tail and two little ones.' The museum was recorded by the 1906 form occupants with this comment: 'In our form room we have a museum – there are two alligators, coins and a lot of other things.' But the most exotic item was recorded in 1907 with this entry from Upper 1: 'Dorothy Collins' father gave us an Australian duck mole' (presumably a duck-billed platypus). None of the 'museum' exhibits have survived, except for the crocodile, now in the care of Mrs Martin, who rescued it from the school dustbin in the early 1990s.

"We thought we would start a museum. Miss Purdie gave us… two snakes which are poisonous…Then somebody gave a beautiful crocodile with a lovely long tail and two little ones."

The contents of the form notice boards have not changed so much since those early days. Form 3 recorded that 'We have two notice boards in the room on either side of the mantelpiece. On one there is a list of our examinations, a temperature chart, a physical record (this was a list, updated once a week after an inspection, of each girl's health and neatness of appearance), and a list of the school rules. On the other, there is a list of the monitresses, the form motto, the time table and the scheme of work.'

Boarding

THE NEED FOR A BOARDING FACILITY was met before 1901 by accommodating a small number of boarders in the Headmistress's quarters on the school premises. This Headmistress's House covered the three floors at the south end of the main school corridor, but sharing this with boarders was not very satisfactory, so in 1901 a house at 11 Higher Summerlands in Heavitree Road was taken, to house between 15 and 18 boarders, with the Clerk's Office eventually becoming established next door at number 10. In 1912, a new house, Tregear, adjacent to main school, was put up for sale by its owner, Mr Simpson, who had made his fortune by inventing the coin-operated utility meter. The opportunity to expand the school site was seized by the Governors, who paid £3,350 for Tregear and turned it into another boarding house for the School. The original boarding house at Summerlands continued to grow and in 1912, when the number of boarders there reached 24, the boarding facilities had to overflow into number 10. In 1913, however, all the Summerland boarders were moved out to the Tregear house. The Headmistress, Miss Trenerry, wrote in the school magazine: 'A great event in the school year was the removal of the Boarding House from Summerland House to Tregear. Not only were the boarders delighted with the house, by its size, its luxuries, and its proximity to the School, but we have all benefited by another Tennis Court.' One of the 'new' boarders wrote: 'It was very exciting trying to find our way about, and each new arrival had to be piloted over the house and shown her dormitory and cubicle, and the way to get to them.'

Summerlands Boarding House

But the increasing demand for boarding places was such that Tregear then had to overflow into the Headmistress' quarters in main school, known as School House, which was back to the original pre-1901 boarding arrangements. In 1914 Mary Westall wrote: 'Our numbers were growing so fast that we were able to be formed into two houses, some living at the School House with Miss Trenerry, but the majority remaining at Tregear. We all formed one 'crocodile' on the walks and were very proud of its length. When we were all in step we sounded like a mighty army'.

Between 1913 and 1919 there were no boarders at Summerlands and it seems to have been rented out to the Exeter Modern School during the First World War. Boarders were moved back into Summerlands from School House after 1919. Boarders from the three houses wrote occasional newsletters to the magazine, and the residence of some French and German language staff at Summerlands led to an 'improving' new development at mealtimes. One of the boarders wrote: 'If the Boarders do not become good linguists, it will not be the fault of Miss Kemp, Miss Taylor and Fraulein Wendt. We have two tables in the Dining Room, one French and one German. The French table is presided over by Miss Kemp, and the German one by Mrs Clarke, Miss Taylor and Fraulein Wendt. At meals, French or German must be spoken except at weekends. Our vain efforts are sometimes very amusing, but we always have someone to turn to for help'.

Tregear and its garden in 1925

Betty Beviss was a boarder who arrived in autumn 1919: 'Life seemed very strange at first, especially after being taught at home. The Head Girl was very awe-inspiring, with hair 'up' and wearing a longish skirt and school blouse. Apart from a few 'bobs' most of the girls had long hair worn in plaits.'

The life of a boarder was well regimented – a bell would ring each morning to get the girls up, followed by prayers on the landing before breakfast. In the evenings, boarders would change out of their gym tunics into ordinary clothes and occupy their time usefully, usually with a game or some handicraft or other, for example, 'sitting on the drawing-room floor sewing while Miss Goodman [Housemistress] read to us'. Bedtime is recorded as, variously, 7.30pm to 9pm for juniors, and 9pm, with lights out at 10pm, for seniors. Exercise too was very important: 'We went for endless walks in croc., and our names were called during supper. We each had to give the amount of exercise taken during the day.' Another girl recalled: 'In 1923 we had a new Housemistress and Matron. Mrs Wood had lived for many years in India, and her dog Butcha soon became one of the family. He joined us on our walks, wearing little boots on wet days ... '

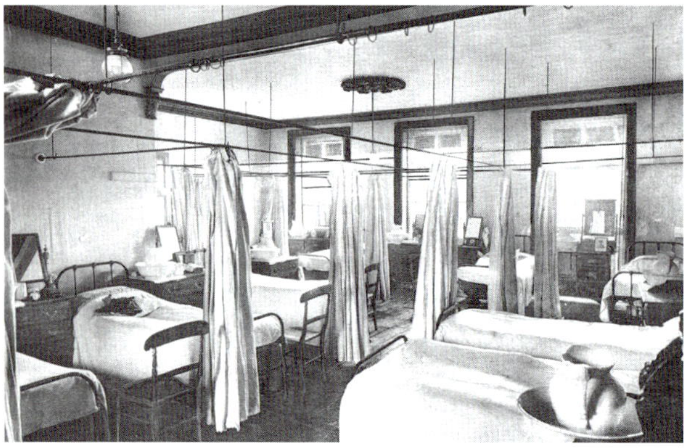

Large dormitory at Summerlands

On Saturdays, outings would be arranged, to Dawlish or Exmouth maybe, or inland to Haldon or Dunsford. Older girls could go out into town or to the cinema as long as they were escorted and later, in the 1940s, house prefects were allowed bicycles, 'When we were allowed bicycles we used to cycle to Topsham and have tea at a funny little café which supplied us with buttered toast and bright pink sticky meringues'. Sports matches played on Saturdays were an alternative amusement. Sundays revolved around attending church; walking in a crocodile to either the Cathedral or St Leonard's Church attired in best suits and hats, 'On Sunday mornings we walked to the Cathedral wearing, in the winter, navy suits, or greatcoats if very cold, and black velour hats, and in summer white dresses and coats, or suits, white panama hats, black shoes and stockings (wool in winter, lisle in summer). If there was any sign of rain we carried black umbrellas.'

In Tregear there were five dormitories, four containing seven beds each; the fifth with four beds. Around each bed was a curtain which could be drawn to make a small cubicle. Nicola Coke recalled her Tregear days in the late 20s/early 30s: '... each cubicle had curtains which we closed modestly when dressing. Each cubicle had also a wash-hand-stand, with jug and basin. Real maids brought real hot water in the mornings, emptied last night's slops, and filled each jug with the day's hot water. We made our own beds, turning the mattress daily beneath the stern eye of a matron. This worthy also used to administer a nasty gargle every night, and a teaspoonful of Syrup of Figs on Fridays. You opened your mouth, in it went, and no nonsense. As for the gargle, you sang loudly and spat vigorously if, like me, you were law-abiding, but the rebels sang and spat while the gargle went unobtrusively from mug to basin by the direct, non-stop route.' Baths were taken every other night and Matron or her assistant washed each girl's hair once a fortnight but brushed it every night. If a girl needed a haircut she would be escorted by Matron to the visiting hairdresser.

"I want it placed on record how well fed we were... the highlight of the week was Sunday lunch when there was a bowl of clotted cream on each table, in winter for the plum pudding, in summer for the apple pie."

Nicola was complimentary about the food: '... I want it placed on record how well fed we were: there was always more than plenty, and the highlight of the week was Sunday lunch when there was a bowl of clotted cream on each table, in winter for the plum pudding, in summer for the apple pie. And on 'Stir Up' Sunday a great mixing bowl was placed in the hall, and every one of us gave a ritual stir to the Christmas pudding.'

Boarding life relaxed somewhat after the Second World War, probably because when Tregear reopened after the bomb damage had been repaired most of the girls were new, as were the boarding house staff, and they had no Sixth Formers, which initially made discipline rather difficult. 'We had cubicle curtains at first, but as we never drew them and used the rails for unlawful purposes they were soon removed. We had our fair share of midnight feasts and dormitory fights, several of us washing our hair before breakfast to remove a glutinous mixture of flour and water. We had memorable end-of-term parties which became quite famous throughout the School, because we had a marvellous cook, and all our day-girl friends hoped for an invitation.'

It was truly the end of an era when, in the early 1960s, the new Headmistress, Miss Bradley, decided to phase out the boarding facility in Tregear (boarding at Summerlands had ended after it was destroyed in the wartime bombing). This had been considered by the previous Head, Miss Ryan, but had been discounted on grounds of cost. Miss Bradley asked for a loan of £27,500 from the St John's Hospital Trust, and the conversion work began in the summer holidays of 1964 after the last boarders had left. Miss Bradley wrote at the time: '... Now new sounds pour forth from Tregear's uncurtained windows. Inside, walls have been removed to make three large L-shaped rooms along the north and west of the house. These will be used for two Art rooms and a Cookery room at the top; nowhere in England will a Cookery room have such a wonderful view! Chapter three is in the process of being written while Tregear stands sadly out of bounds to its friends over in the School. By this time next year chapter four will have opened when Tregear will have once again been invaded by Maynardians with a difference, for this time they will all be day-girls'. While it is clear that everything possible was done to keep disruption to a minimum it should not be underestimated how difficult many Maynardians of the time found this change. Boarder Gillian Dobie wrote: 'It seems unbelievable to think that the next time many of us, the 'final' boarders, will have a chance to revisit the School, Tregear, which has been our term-time home for so long, will consist of such things as classrooms, domestic science rooms, and music rooms. We gradually became used to the fact that summer term would be everyone's last term in Tregear. Early on in the term prospective buyers started coming to be shown round the house. Then items of furniture started disappearing, and what was left became adorned with small pieces of paper stating 'sold'. By the end of term even the beds weren't really ours to sleep in, and we had to get out in the mornings onto bare floorboards rather than rugs. One of the saddest occasions was at the Grand Fête in July. The lawn outside Tregear, and the rooms leading onto it, were absolutely packed with items for sale – our chairs, our tables, our mirrors ... We are very grateful to Mrs Laird, Matron and Cook, who brought Tregear to its close with the minimum of fuss and bother, and disturbed us as little as possible – a fact appreciated by the O- and A-level candidates. A lot of girls are going to miss a lot of things with the closing of Tregear. No more 7.30 bells, no more lining up for cough medicine, slinking away from confiscations, and holding marvellous midnight feasts ... Tregear will always be pictured in our minds as the boarding house, and the friendly life that went with it.'

Tregear boarders having a sing-song, c1955

Despite things like the initiation ceremony of 'lamb singing', an ordeal that in the 1940s every new girl had to undergo: 'that is, standing on a chair and singing a song to the whole house – once that was over things definitely improved!', boarders, on the whole, appreciated and valued their years in Tregear '... discipline was strict, and the routine of daily life was regular, and we learned loyalty to a small community. Looking back, I find all this was a safe and understandable framework in which to grow.'

But perhaps the essence of boarding life in Tregear is best summed up by Sheila Fawkner-Corbett (Lake) remembering her days in the late 1940s: 'When there was any function on at School, the boarders were always expected to act as general dogsbodies, a fact which we rather resented, but no doubt it was character-forming! And how we enjoyed the last few days of term, when boarding house as well as school discipline was relaxed. Excitement ran high when the trunks were brought into the dormitories, and the delight in packing them and tying them up; then they were piled in the hall prior to being collected by the railway van. At last, the end of term, the agony of cramming all those odds and ends into too-small cases, and the thrill of stripping the beds, and the final good-byes until next term. How I hated coming back, but how I enjoyed it once I was there!'

The school day

AUDREY JONES (Etheridge, 1939–45) has rather painful memories of Morning Assembly: 'Everyone – including staff – knelt for the prayers, and the floor surface wasn't too kind in those days. It was not good for lisle stockings [cotton knit stockings that tended to wrinkle] which were the order of the day. (Nylons hadn't been heard of then).' Even up until the 1960s, each form entered the hall in a carefully defined order, having waited lined up in silence in the corridor for its turn to enter; prefects entered onto the platform via what was then the Biology lab, led by the Head Girl along the top of the platform, where they remained for the duration of assembly. 'Once a week class lists would be read out, including people who had Order Marks or other detentions. Each house gathered afterwards and discussions took place. Awards like carriage girdles, gym badges, sports badges, etc., were all presented at assembly, and results of inter-school matches were announced and mention given to any outstanding performance. On being mentioned three times for any one particular sport a badge would be awarded – one to sew on the tunic and one for the blazer pocket.'

Even as late as the 1960s the Headmistress wore an academic gown to assembly, and at the end, as the classes filed out, pupils with sickness absence notes and requests from parents for time out of School would queue at the headmistress's table on the stage to present their parents' letters.

End-of-term assembly was always eagerly awaited, just as it is today! It was, and remains, an occasion when pupils' awards and prizes were given out. Fiona Dawrant remembers particularly one end-of-term assembly in 1979: 'There were many tears shed by pupils when Miss Bradley left'.

Little is known about the structure of the school day in the Maynard's early beginnings but, by the time the establishment had moved to its present site, a school day had been established, the timings being very similar to those in place today.

Starting the day with callisthenics in the early 1900s

Between 1891 and 1901, when Miss Turner was in charge, the school day started at 9.15am and continued until 1.15pm. Lunch and callisthenics (a Swedish exercise drill) then followed and from 3–4pm there was optional supervised preparation for lessons.

By 1939 the school hours were 9am until 12.50pm, resuming after lunch from 2.20pm until 3.40 or 4pm dependent on the age group. A decade later the school day was starting earlier at 8.45am, although Junior Department was closed on Wednesday afternoons. As a junior, Mary Ellis recalls an embarrassing day when she turned up (after having lunch at home as usual) for a session, only to be told that it was Wednesday and she had to go home again!

The school day included lunch, which was served to most of the pupils. In the 1930s, pupils ate in the dining room, partitioned off from the teachers' dining room. A prefect was assigned to each table to ensure order was kept. The discipline was quite strict – if water was spilt by a pupil, she was not allowed any more that lunchtime; if the pupils were too noisy, a bell was rung, and from then on lunch was eaten in silence.

Susan Allison (Burdett, 1947–56) recalls: 'Miss Ryan would process down the centre of the hall and lead prayers and hymns before we marched back to our classrooms for lessons: two before break of 15 minutes, two before lunch, break until 2.10pm, then two more lessons. Some children had to leave at 3.30 pm to catch buses home, but the rest of us finished at 3.40pm. Homework had to be given in each morning and taken down in sets to the staff pigeonholes on the ground floor. Only half the School could have cooked dinner each day so we brought packed lunches on alternate days and ate them in the school hall. We had to buy dinner tickets (8d [3p today] I seem to remember) and hand them in before dinner. There was an upstairs dining room as well. There was no choice in either of the two courses. The teacher on duty would come round and inspect our plates after each course and there was a prefect on each table. Miss Anderson, the Classics teacher, always said grace in Latin, '*Benedictus, benedicat, Dominum nostrum, Jesum Christum*'.

Essentially, lunchtimes in the 1960s were little changed from the 1930s, with a Sixth Former still assigned to each table to keep order. Lyn Hope (Lynda Bayley, 1958–65) remembers, 'We sat at the same table all year with two prefects serving out the lunch. There was no choice of food but it wasn't too bad – treacle pudding or 'school stodge' as we called it, was a particular favourite. Wednesday was not a good day for me as we always had liver with mashed potato and carrots followed by rice pudding. A member of staff sat at the first table and said grace. The rest of the staff sat at a table at the end of the room.'

The discipline was quite strict – if water was spilt by a pupil, she was not allowed any more that lunchtime; if the pupils were too noisy, a bell was rung, and from then on lunch was eaten in silence.

'Break times and lunchtimes were spent outside unless the weather was really bad. A notice saying **'Recreation Out'** or **'Recreation In'** was displayed downstairs. I can remember shivering in the bike sheds many times. We were allowed to go into the main hall sometimes during cold or wet weather and this always seemed a special treat. At break time we had buns. These were in the dining hall (where Pring is today) and we had to give in a ticket from the Bun Book bought at the beginning of term. Miss Flemington, the Domestic Bursar, stood at the entrance and collected the tickets. If you were quick you might get a doughnut, although my favourites were Chelsea buns. I remember the half-drunk bottles of milk littering the walls at the end of break.'

Freda Jackson remembers that when she entered the School in 1950, aged 11, the weekly timetable consisted of seven periods per day – six lessons of English, four lessons of French, Maths and PE, two lessons of Geography, History, RE and Music and one free period. In addition there were double periods of Science, Art, Craft and Needlework, in which her class's first project was to make a pair of knickers by hand, using school summer dress material. Bridget Kirby (Pearse, 1946–1957) also recalls making a pair of knickers from parachute silk. In the early-50s 'dip pens' were still used for written work in School, though many girls used fountain pens for homework, but in 1952, with Miss Underdown as their form mistress – her first year at the Maynard – Freda's class was officially allowed to use fountain pens at School. Ballpoint pens were still a novelty at this time.

As today, the school timetable was arranged so that most staff had one afternoon a week when they were not obliged to be in School. The difference then was that on these days, in place of staff who were form mistresses, Sixth Form prefects were allocated a particular class, and would be in the relevant classroom at the start of the afternoon session, keeping order(?!), and calling the Register.

Gill Newport, a pupil in the 1960s, remembers that lesson bells were rung by the prefects in the Sixth Form using a hand-held bell. The bell was rung both inside and outside to ensure everyone had heard it, and it was a great privilege to perform this duty.

In the early 1990s school registration commenced a little earlier at 8.40am followed by an assembly attended by a mixture of different forms on different days. The lesson bells were by now on an automated system and lunchtimes were less regulated than in the past, with only a lunch mistress employed to oversee that the girls behaved in an orderly manner. Those who attended clubs at lunchtime could obtain a priority pass, as is still the case – these were sometimes fraudulently obtained to cover as many days as possible. Good manners and eating etiquette were expected and, in the Junior School, good manners were occasionally taught in assembly.

With Dr West's arrival in 2000 the school day changed its format slightly in that the assembly was moved to the afternoon, thus making the morning six periods long with two periods in the afternoon so that more lessons could be taught as double periods. In addition, a five-minute changeover period between lessons was brought in to reduce the mad scramble in trying to be in two places at once.

Drama productions

EARLY PRODUCTIONS WERE QUITE LOW-KEY AFFAIRS performed by just a few. The 1902 school magazine notes: '*The Rivals* was successfully acted one evening by members of the Literary Society. The play was a great success, and gave quite as much enjoyment to the actors themselves as to the spectators.' In 1909 'A scene from Euripides Alcestis was successfully acted by F Griffith, A Booker and L von Arnim. Also German songs and a performance of La Tortue et les Deux Canards, a French fable.'

The Old Girls had their own Dramatic Society and also mounted regular productions, sometimes jointly with the School, for example: 'Four performances of *Antigone of Sophocles*, performed by members of School and Old Girls', in 1914.

1921 production of *Quality Street*

With Miss Dixon's arrival in 1920 the expansion of school activities included theatre trips; one to see a famous contemporary actor, Frank Benson in *The Rivals*; and on another occasion, organising a visit from playwright Mr St John Ervine, to give a talk to the school's Dramatic Society. Amateur dramatics became an exciting feature of the School, and a staff/student production of a play called *Quality Street* was staged in 1921. A Junior School pupil wrote a report for the school magazine of 1922: 'We had a play. It was called Quality Street. Miss Macferson took the chief part with Miss Haigh-Brown. Miss Gregison looked after all the dresses, and they were sweet and lovly coulers [sic]. Most of the staff were in it and two girls out of our Form, and some of the prefects too. It was very nice because everybody put so much expression in it. The children's faces were made up with lipstick very nicely and made them look better, and it was a very nice ending to it.'

Productions became increasingly ambitious over the years, involving more and more members of the School, and in January 1924 'School produced Sir James Barrie's play *A Kiss for Cinderella*.' In 1936 *Hansel & Gretel*, an 'operatic drama' was the highlight of the year. As with so much else, drama productions were put on hold during the war years, *Antigone*, in 1949, being the first production after the War. This must have been quite an undertaking and seemed to set the tone for the next few years, as in 1953: 'One of the most outstanding events of the School Year was the production of *Iphigenia in Tauris,* which was much enjoyed by all who took part, and acclaimed by the audience as a fitting sequel to *Antigone*'. Again, in 1956, 'the School, according to custom, produced a Greek play. This year Mrs Lloyd chose Gilbert Murray's translation of the *Alcestis of Euripides*, with music written for it by Gustav Holst.'

1958 was, of course, the Tercentenary year, so, to celebrate, the School gave a major performance of Dryden's *King Arthur*, with music by Purcell.

By the late 60s/early 70s a variety of different performances was being prepared each year, some within year groups, some written by the girls themselves and some produced jointly with other schools. For example, *The Dragon* was produced with Exeter School, in 1969, along with an Upper Sixth production of *Arsenic and Old*

1949 production of *Antigone*

Lace and 'To close the year, the Upper 5s provided us with two short, but entertaining plays. The first, a mystery entitled *Dark Brown* … The second … a review *Chains and Changes* was written by members of the cast, with the theme of the "enormous changes that have taken place in the School since about 1900."' This featured an impersonation of the school caretaker, Mr Harris, and it could have been a forerunner of the present-day Sixth Form entertainment on the last day of the autumn term when events and personalities of the past school year are lampooned to (almost) universal delight.

During 1972 the Sixth Form made several outings to the Northcott Theatre to see a variety of different performances and, by the end of 1987, Maynard productions had been placed firmly on the map with a three-day production of *Salad Days* at the Barnfield Theatre, followed by, in December 1989, an enormously successful production of *Daisy Pulls It Off*, also at the Barnfield.

Drama productions, of one sort or another, remain an important part of Maynard life, complemented nowadays by events like the English Department's unmissable trip to Stratford each year when the girls, having been immersed in all things Shakespearian for several days, always come back buzzing with new insights and ideas.

A scene from the 1958 (Tercentenary) production of *King Arthur*

Music and concerts

As with drama, the musical life (particularly performing) of the Maynard started in a small way in 1902 when Dr Wood, Music Master at the Maynard and Organist at Exeter Cathedral, started a School Orchestra with just 20 members. It wasn't a very encouraging beginning as the 1904 school magazine reported that, 'Dr Wood considers the work of the Orchestra as a whole is promising, but at present no very difficult music can be attempted', and by 1905 the Orchestra had dropped to a mere nine members. Despite this 'it was decided to give two or three concerts of purely Chamber Music at the High School. The first concert was given on November 30th, 1905, and consisted of string quartettes [sic] by Haydn and Mozart, a violin solo by Bach, and songs by each of the three composers. The second concert was given on March 20th, 1906. The works performed were string quartettes of Mendelssohn and Schumann, besides several charming songs contributed by Dr Wood's Singing Class. We very much hope that this may be the beginning of an annual series of Chamber Music Concerts given at the High School during the winter months.' From then on concerts or recitals of some sort happened on a regular, but maybe not frequent, basis.

Musically speaking, 1929 was a big year for the Maynard as '… the Exeter Philharmonic Society's concerts took place in the Maynard School Hall. These concerts were a great treat to those Maynardians who, by means of a specially reduced season ticket, were able to hear such distinguished musicians as the Spencer Dyke Quartette [string quartet], Myra Hess [pianist], Clara Serena [contralto] and Roy Mellish [her accompanist and husband] and, lastly, Senor [Gaspar] Cassado [cellist].' These were all top musicians of their day and it's amazing to think of them performing in our School hall. A similar arrangement is recorded in the 'Music in School' section of the 1944/45 magazine: 'Continuing to flourish as the centre of musical interest in the School, the Subscription Concerts now enter their third season. The artistes have played to a full hall, and on more than one occasion have remarked on the appreciative character of their audience; an audience consisting of friends and visitors, and an increasing percentage of Maynardians.' In the same year the School also mounted a production of Purcell's Opera, *Dido & Aeneas*.

Maynard Choir of 1946 just after winning a competition at Crediton

Music making and performing were now gathering momentum as, in 1946, it was reported that the 'The Choir gave several outside performances' and in the following year that: 'Violin classes are going to be started if sufficient people are interested … the choir is already practising for a Christmas Concert.' In 1949 the School Orchestra was revived after a lapse of many years, 'the members being that small group of people in the School who can play an instrument apart from the piano', and the School entered both a Senior and Junior Choir in the Devon Music Festival, the former gaining a first in the sight-reading section, and the latter tying for second place in their section.

By 1970 a whole range of musical activities and achievements, both curricular and extra-curricular, were an intrinsic element of Maynard life: 'We were very pleased to be able to re-establish lessons in the classical guitar. Miss Murray started regular rehearsals of chamber music for wind instruments, two groups entering for the Devon and Exeter Music Festival ... The Senior Choir retained the Ross Cup, and the Fourth Form Choir won the Chichester Shield. The Madrigal Group gained 90 marks and an Honours Certificate. Following a suggestion by Clare Portman, a House Music Festival was organised during the spring term. Each House was able to present a good, varied programme within the time limit of 15 minutes ... The Exeter City Library invited us to give a concert in the Music Room there on 7th May ... Later the Madrigal Group was invited to take part in a concert in aid of the St Nicholas Home.'

In May 1972 the highlight of a highly successful school concert was *Joseph and the Amazing Technicolour Dreamcoat*, 'sung by the Fourth Form Choir, accompanied by a small orchestra.' A long-playing record (LP) was made of this together with the first movements of both a Mozart Flute Concerto, and a Bach Concerto for oboe and violin, as well as Bizet's March from Carmen. In 1974 a second LP was made featuring performances of *Captain Noah and his Floating Zoo* at the Barnfield Theatre in 1973 and Vivaldi's *Gloria* at the University Great Hall in 1974.

As with Drama productions, joint performances started to be arranged – Gilbert and Sullivan's *Trial by Jury* at the Barnfield Theatre with Exeter School in 1973; Mendelssohn's *Elijah* in Exeter Cathedral with the combined choirs of the Maynard, St Margaret's and Exeter Schools in 1975; a joint production with Blundell's of Purcell's *Dido & Aeneas* at the Barnfield in 1976 and Gilbert and Sullivan's *Iolanthe*, again with Blundell's at the Barnfield, in 1977. Also in the early 1970s, the Carol Concert was held in St Matthew's Church for the first time.

In 1982 a Choral Society was started, made up mostly of parents, its first concert being the Fauré Requiem in Exeter Cathedral. The Choral Society continued until 1992 when its demise seems to have been the only downbeat note in an otherwise busy and fulfilling year, 'In October we staged the School's first full-scale autumn concert. More concerts have become necessary to accommodate the greater amount of practical musical activity taking place in School. This year we were invited, for the first time, to take part in the Exeter Festival ... with a lunchtime recital in The Mint Methodist Church in June, featuring Middle School Choir, the clarinet group and soloists Rachel Barber (oboe) and Cathy Longman (soprano). After a number of years of forming an ad hoc orchestra to accompany the Choral Society, a Chamber Orchestra was formally organised to perform music in its own right and give a further opportunity for more advanced string players. The Music department has seen some reorganisation this year, as a temporary measure before Tregear is redeveloped for Art and Music. The main music room has been relocated to the old Needlework room, providing more much needed space for class music teaching. Tregear cloakrooms, now no longer needed for their original purpose, have been colonised with a piano for class lessons in composition ... On the downside, support for the Choral Society has fallen–causing us for the first time in 10 years to cancel their annual performance of a major choral work in the Spring Concert.'

Phase 1 of the redevelopment of Tregear was completed in 1995, the same year as the arrival of the School's first music scholar and recipients of music bursaries. The turn of the millennium was marked by a number of new and exciting achievements, '... in November 1999 we held our first Music Open Day inviting Year Six pupils from schools across Devon to join with our own young musicians in a day of music making ... The summer term brought even greater excitement! First there was our participation in the BBC's national 'Music Live' event, for which Maynard Musicians gave an hour-long broadcast from Main School Hall,' and 'the Chamber Choir ... gained a place in the finals of the National Choral competition at the South Bank's Queen Elizabeth Hall.'

During 2008, the 350th anniversary was marked, at Exeter Cathedral, with a truly breathtaking Gala Concert involving over 200 Maynard musicians, and a Thanksgiving Service at which the Chamber Choir sang so movingly; accounts of these appear later in this book. Suffice to say that the Maynard without Music is unthinkable!

Junior Maynardian, Anastasia Bruce-Jones, practising her violin, 2007

Clubs, societies and activities

THE MAYNARD SCHOOL HAS ALWAYS OFFERED a wide range of extra-curricular activity, the earliest specific reference being the first meeting of the Camera Club in 1907, 'The prize for the "Church" was divided between Mildred Veitch and Dorothy Harris.' Photography competitions were held twice a year and were open to the entire School. In 1911 a lecture entitled 'Photography as a Hobby' was given to the group. It is clear that there was a great deal of interest in photography within the School at this time, which would coincide with it becoming available to a mass market with the development of hand-held box cameras and ready-made gelatine dry plates.

Also around this time there was a strong tradition of gardening within the School, with girls responsible for cultivating their own little plots. An entry in the 1912 school magazine indicates that gardening was taken very seriously, 'The principal criticism to be made is that though the Gardens were on the whole very bright with flowers, the gardening was too intermittent – seeds were not sown, and not regularly watered, sweet pea was planted and not staked, and there was not enough constant weeding or tidying, or cutting off of withered flowers.'

"...though the Gardens were on the whole very bright with flowers, the gardening was too intermittent..."

'The best Garden was that of Frances Clogg, Mary Anderson and Margaret Gadd. This, on the whole was well and steadily cared for, with the exception that the withered flowers and seed vessels were not always removed. The second was that of Marjorie Mainwaring, which was regularly and carefully kept, though there might have been more systematic weeding. Third came that of Sybil Preedy, who also took a great interest in it, and had several very nice plants. The garden of Dorothy Cummings and Norah Ross would have been very good, if they had not relaxed their efforts. They had some good plants, and very carefully prepared the ground for the sweet pea, which would, in consequence, have been very fine plants if they had been properly staked.'

'There has been great interest taken in gardening this autumn; there are now twenty-five gardens, and many bulbs have been put down, so we hope to have a good display of flowers in the coming Spring.'

Over the years various clubs and societies have come and gone or developed in other ways, a reflection of their time, a perfect example being the renaming of the Sixth Form's Post War Society to Forum in 1970, 'its aims were reviewed and revised in accordance with the state of affairs in the world today.' Other societies reported in the early 70s were Modern Languages, History, Literary, Scientific, Photographic, Junior Dramatic, Geography Field Club, Craft Club, Junior Biology Club and both Senior and Junior Christian Union. In 1976 the Sixth Form started a Careers Society and in 1979 the Chess Society was resurrected, 'Much to our amazement, the response to the revitalised Chess Society was very enthusiastic ...', as was the Debating Society.

In 1987 a Theatre Club was started 'to provide a full and varied programme of theatrical entertainment for pupils, parents, staff and friends of the School.' This seems to have been very successful as during the year 1989–90 members of the club saw a huge number of productions: *42nd Street* and *Chess* at the Theatre Royal, Plymouth; *Beyond Reasonable Doubt* and *Lady Windermere's Fan* at the Bristol Hippodrome; *Cats, Shadowlands, Jeffrey Barnard is Unwell, Miss Saigon, Sunday Night in the Park with George*, all in London, and a Kenneth Branagh Shakespeare double bill at the Bath Theatre Royal. A Ballroom Dancing Club, started by Miss Glanville in 1988, seems to have equally successful as, by 1990, it had 100 members.

These days there is a wealth of extra-curricular activities on offer including many different sports, language clubs and music clubs. In addition Sixth Formers run a variety of clubs for the Junior Department, examples in 2008 being French, Reading, Cookery, Art, and 'Awesome Antics', an offshoot of the Christian Union. Sixth Formers and junior girls alike gain enormous enjoyment from their involvement with these clubs.

School uniform

THE EARLIEST 'UNIFORMS' WERE THE BLUE GOWNS worn by the poor girls attending the very first charitable foundation, which were the reason that it became known at the Blue Maids' Hospital. The Hospital received various bequests from time to time and one of these was from a Gilbert Keate 'towards the maintenance of two boys and two maids … it was also directed that the said children should wear on the sleeves of their hospital gowns the letters G K'. Another early reference is in one of the Minute Books of the Blue Maids' School, dated 1711: '… ordered that Gowns and Pettycoats be provided'. This 'uniform' echoed that of the Blue Boys – a blue gown and cap – and some small cast metal painted statues were made depicting a Blue Boy, one of which stood in the entrance to the main hall of the St John's Hospital School in the High Street. In January 1996 the Governors of St John's Hospital Educational Foundation presented an original Blue Boy statue to the Maynard to mark the School's longstanding and continuing connection with St John's Hospital. There are three other versions known to be in existence: one (unpainted) at the Royal Albert Memorial Museum; the one from St John's Hospital School standing in Princesshay, close to its original home; and a third at Exeter School which has also long benefited from St John's Hospital funding.

It appears that at some point a uniform of cherry and straw colours was adopted but the dates are unknown. The 1902 school magazine records, in its 'Notes of the Year': 'The old school colours – cherry and straw – appeared to have died out entirely. More serviceable colours being needed for the various purposes required by the Games Club – blouses, ties, hatbands, &c. – dark blue, light blue and white were chosen in their place.'

Form 2 in 1927/28 showing off their uniform

In the 1920s the few boys in Junior School wore their own clothes – shorts, ties, shirts and sweaters – but they had to look neat and tidy. The girls wore pleated tunics tied with a navy blue girdle, or light grey dresses with lace collars. The girls who wore tunics had either a large collar, which could be lacey, or a small rounded collar over the top of their tunics. With the smaller collar they wore a cravat-style tie. On their tunics the girls could have a sew-on house badge. School hats were compulsory – navy blue velour in the winter; boaters, or later, panama hats in the summer, both with the school badge on. Rules regarding shoes were very strict. Outdoor shoes had to be black and lace-up, whilst indoors rubber-soled shoes with a strap had to be worn. The black lace-ups were worn to School, with galoshes over the top of them in wet weather, changing into the indoor shoes immediately on arrival at School. Girls had two pairs of gym shoes: black ones for gym and white ones which had to be whitened every time before they were used. For sport, juniors wore blue shorts and a shirt and senior girls wore blue aertex dresses for gym, these being a new part of the uniform in the 1930s. The tunic continued in some form for several decades, and by the 1950s was being worn with a long-sleeved blouse, white with a thin navy stripe, and a tie that was navy with wide diagonal black stripes edged in pale blue. Lower 5 and upwards wore the same blouse and tie, but with a skirt rather than a tunic. Tunics had to be three inches above the knee when kneeling and this was checked at the beginning of every term by the PE staff. Girls could also wear a navy v-neck jumper that had a blue stripe at the waist, wrist and neck, but cardigans were not allowed. The fabric for the blouses had to be purchased and these made up, as ready-made school blouses were not yet available in the shops. The juniors wore white ankle or navy knee-length socks and the seniors black stockings. Outer garments were a navy

Old and new uniforms in 1962, Miss Bradley's first year as Head. Stephanie Vine entering Lower 1 in her, and the School's, new uniform: dark navy waisted tunic dress, white shirt with a fine dark blue stripe and a 'very itchy collar', and striped tie. Jennifer, Stephanie's older sister, is wearing the old-style uniform – the shapeless tunic tied with a fabric girdle. In Kindergarten and Transition Stephanie had not been required to wear uniform.

blue raincoat and school hat, which around the crown had a wide striped ribbon of navy, pale blue and black, was embroidered with the school badge, and which 'you took off outside School at your own risk (of being reported and reprimanded in School)'. The two pairs of black shoes, one for outdoor use, and one for indoor use only, were still part of the uniform but Susan Allison remembers in the immediate post-war years having to 'dye sandals when only brown ones were available.' The summer uniform was a dress, in a tiny blue, white and navy check, to a standard pattern, a navy blazer with the school badge on the pocket, and a Panama hat with band and school badge. In 1972 it was decided to dispense altogether with the hat: 'The varied hairstyles of the younger members of the School are now in evidence throughout Exeter, owing to the recent abolition of hats as part of the school uniform.'

By the 1990s the winter school uniform had become a contentious issue. A record card in early-1991 states: 'Various comments made by Staff & Pupils about the present winter uniform, resulted in a SURVEY carried out last term for Staff. The survey revealed that the majority of staff were not happy with the uniform & felt that all the garments should be investigated. It was agreed that we try to find WARMER, BETTER QUALITY, COMFORTABLE, & PRACTICAL garments for the 1990s. The SKIRT in particular was too easily adapted according to FASHION. The Courtelle jumper was not warm enough for some pupils. The tie was an inconvenience & an added expense.'

The 'new' uniform agreed upon was, for juniors: Black Watch tartan tunic or a full, permanently-pleated skirt, both made from acrylic/wool, with a white shirt, round-necked navy raglan-sleeve jumper in wool/nylon or Courtelle, and navy tights, a navy duffle coat, and blazer. The uniform for the seniors became a Black Watch tartan kilt, same fabric as the tunic, with a white shirt, and jumper, tights and blazer or duvet-type coat in navy blue.

This uniform has remained essentially the same since then, albeit with occasional changes of detail but, most importantly, a lighter-weight softer fabric for the kilts so that older girls can now wear the kilt and blouse all year round.

In the early 1940s, the scarlet Shoe Bags had to be made, often by the girls, to a fiendishly difficult pattern supplied by the School: 'It comprised two pockets; one for gym shoes, one for house shoes'. By the 70s the Shoe Bag appears to have acquired a wider use '...containing the mandatory items, namely science overall, white aertex shirt, wrap-round games skirt, black plimsolls, black hockey boots and royal blue hockey socks.'

The carriage girdle crops up repeatedly in Old Maynardians' recollections. This was a soft grey 6cm-wide sash worn around the waist instead of the standard navy sash, and denoted an award for good deportment. Carriage girdles were re-awarded each term and were evidently highly-prized.

The Sixth Formers wore black silk stockings with their uniform. In the early years prefects wore boaters in the summer and Wren-style tricorne felt hats in the winter, the latter being brought in sometime after 1935, when, apparently, boaters could no longer be obtained. These hats clearly caused quite a stir because in 1947 the national *Daily Mirror* newspaper ran a story about them: 'When fellow travellers on Exeter trains ask girls in Wren officers "uniform" where they are stationed they blush and say: "At school." "Even a Royal Marine asked me where I was based", red-headed Wendy Sykes told the *Daily Mirror* yesterday. "He was amazed to find I was a schoolgirl." The confusion arises from the purchase by their headmistress, Miss E M Ryan, of surplus Wren officers' tricorne hats for the prefects of Maynard Girls' School, Exeter. "Now that we can't get straw boaters for the twelve senior girls, we decided the black velour tricornes would be ideal," Miss Ryan said. With their tailored navy greatcoats and black shoes and stockings the girls look very much like Wren officers. Miss Ryan strictly enforces one rule about these hats – they MUST be worn straight.' So these hats, sporting the Maynard school badge where the Navy crest once was, were obviously very distinctive and, by all accounts, proudly worn. The 1956/57 magazine records the revival of straw boaters: 'At popular request, an old custom was revived in the summer term, for, with rather mixed feelings, the prefects abandoned their tricornes for the summer, and bravely set out in boaters. In spite of the consternation of some of the younger citizens of Exeter, it was generally agreed that the idea was a success.' – unlike back in 1913; as Petronella Jones (Snowball) remembered '... the School wore straw boaters. My mother, who like Miss Bradbeer's mother was a law unto herself, said I looked ridiculous in one and bought me a good navy velour and put the school ribbon on it and in the summer a real panama.'

Sixth Form prefects in their Wren-officer tricorne hats, as pictured in the 1947 Daily Mirror.

Sixth Formers wore uniform up until 1970 although early on tunics had at least been replaced with skirts. Lyn Hope remembers: 'We still wore uniform, a stripey blouse, tie and navy skirt and still the shapeless blue summer dress. The summer hat was a panama. By the time I left a hint of rebellion was creeping in (it was the 1960s after all!), and we rolled the brims of the hats up at the sides and wore them on the backs of our heads.' During 1969 it was decided to trial a Sixth Form without uniform. 'Needless to add, for the first few days the School took on the appearance of a fashion house and there were several amusing instances of Sixth Formers being mistaken for members of staff. Now that things have settled down, the overwhelming opinion favours remaining out of uniform, not only for appearance's sake, but also because many feel that it promotes a better relationship between pupils and staff and at least helps to relieve that terrible 'Monday morning' feeling.' The following year the abolition of Sixth Form uniform was firmly established followed in 1972 by a further relaxation of the rules: 'The Sixth Form are now allowed to wear trousers; a fact which has produced mixed feelings amongst the rest of the School, but which is greatly appreciated by the Sixth Form.' These uniform changes must have seemed very radical at the time but were, in fact, reflecting a more general fundamental change that had taken place in 1970 – the lowering of the age of majority to 18. Members of the Upper Sixth could now vote and were officially adults, something that would have been unbelievable to earlier Maynardians like Nellie Tillard, a suffragette who had been imprisoned for her campaigning.

Girls in summer dresses walking up main drive, 1949

Day of Self-Government

In 1969 a 'Day of Self-Government' was started, something it is inconceivable to imagine holding today! 'As an experiment this year, the School was run for one day by the Upper Sixth, with Miss Bradley and two other members of staff in school in case of need. The aim was to make everybody in the School co-operate to accomplish a project. We were given as much freedom as possible in our choice of activities. A group of four or five Upper Sixth worked with one junior form throughout the day. Of the 10 groups, some selected a variety of topics to study during the day, others chose a single overall theme. Many groups included in their timetables some form of self-expression, for instance painting, dance drama and improvisation; others included topics from the traditional school subjects, such as history and physics. Two groups brought in speakers in the afternoon. During the dinner hour Sarah Bush and Felicity Browne arranged a folk-singing session. The experiment was a great success. None of the fears of those who had seen the film *If...* were realised, and nearly everyone enjoyed the day.'

It was repeated in 1970 with, again, only three members of staff on site for the entire day 'in case of emergency' and 'no serious injuries were sustained by school or Sixth Form, apart from nervous exhaustion!'. The Day of Self-Government continued annually until 1980, with, in 1973, an insightful observation from Sixth Former Sara Payne, 'It was a unique opportunity of experiencing the difficulties involved in teaching 30 rather restless girls, and from now on we all no doubt respect the patience of the teaching profession rather more than hitherto.'

Curriculum and achievements

FROM EARLY DAYS, the School offered two alternative curricula: one for those girls working towards public examinations, and one where the emphasis was on domestic and craft subjects, which at the turn of the century included Leather Work, Clay Modelling, Lace Work, Woodcarving and Needlework. Domestic Science was a major subject on the curriculum, with maximum use of the Cookery room established by Miss Trenerry, the School's fourth Head, who in 1908 set up a course for external students working towards the 'Home Workers' Housewifery Certificate'. This involved lessons in Cooking, Laundry work, Dressmaking & Fine Needlework, and Housewifery & Hygiene – an early example of widening access and community use of school facilities. The separate Domestic Science curriculum was still a feature in 1935, when the School offered an initial four-year course in Needlework, followed by a more specialised two-year course in Needlework & Housewifery, offered by the National Council of Domestic Studies.

The other curriculum was for academic courses working towards public examinations set by the universities, although during Miss Hall's headship parents could opt as to whether their daughters would be entered for the exams or just attend lessons. Once in the Sixth Form, girls had a choice of three academic courses: Classics (including Ancient History & Greek Testament), Science & Mathematics, or Humanities. In the first 10 years of the Girls' High School, examination results were excellent. One of the earliest 'Prize Giving' programmes to have survived dates from the last decade of the 19th century. Lady Poltimore was the guest speaker, and she outlined the examination successes of recent years. Individual girls from the School had won the highest examination board mark awarded nationally, one girl for French in 1882, two for Geography in 1884 and 1885 respectively (accompanied by medals from the Royal Geographical Society), and another girl achieved the second highest mark nationally in 1886, so the Geography teaching must have been particularly effective. Another individual had the second highest mark in English in 1884, and two girls came equal second nationally for French in 1886. Lady Poltimore also announced that one pupil had won an open scholarship to Newnham College, Cambridge. An Honours Board, still in place, was set up in the school hall to record past pupils' degree results at the universities they attended once they had left the Maynard School.

Art class in the Main Hall, c1920. Note the hanging gas lamps.

In 1902, when Miss Purdie took over, the curriculum was enlarged. The Cambridge Higher and Local Certificates continued to be taken in the Lower and Upper Sixth. The range of subjects taught was wide and varied: Latin & Literature, Natural Science, Modern Languages, Mathematics, Vocal Music, Domestic Economy & Laws of Health, English, History, Geography, and Art. Girls also fitted in Drawing on Wednesday afternoons, Games on Thursday afternoons and Dancing on Fridays. Professor Sadler, in his report to the Board of Education in 1905, was concerned that the range of subjects offered might prevent pupils from excelling at one. However, this same report commended the teaching of all subjects throughout the School. The lessons were noted as having no 'undue repression' within them! Miss Purdie was very open-minded and encouraged teachers to use innovative methods to improve their teaching. Science was taught heuristically, which means that the girls were encouraged to find out and discover things for themselves through problem-solving. This method, so progressive then, is standard practice in today's schools. Modern languages were taught using 'oral' methods, with the lessons being conducted in the language being taught. This was based on teaching techniques employed in schools on the continent and shows that, from the outset, the Maynard was striving to produce the best education for girls.

In the first decades of the 20th century, the School had established itself as an important centre for teacher training, involving a system of mentoring, whereby a designated member of staff tutored a student teacher in Psychology and Theory of Education, and supervised their teacher training. In 1905, the School was one of only eight establishments nationwide outside London authorised for teacher training under the Teachers' Training Registration Regulations. The importance of this training was recognised in 1906 by Oxford University Teacher Training College, which asked the School to mentor one of their students in a placement at the School for the third term of training, initially the only girls' school to be involved with the University for this system.

The Domestic Science curriculum continued to be a major part of the girls' education. An exercise book of a girl studying for her Housecraft Certificate in 1924 shows the areas that the syllabus covered. In Cooking, diagrams of meat cuts were drawn and identified while, under Infant Care, the relative advantages and disadvantages of bottle feeding were discussed. In the Laundry section the crimping of frills was taught, and in Housewifery the girls were taught which colour wallpaper would best suit certain rooms.

As late as 1931 it is clear that these skills were considered in many quarters to be very important as illustrated by Miss Violet E Wills' words on opening the Maynard's new Domestic Science block in that year. 'I think it [Domestic Science] a very important part of education … A lot of things we learn perhaps we make no use of. I do not, for instance, use Algebra, and it has not fallen to my lot to make any use of the lectures in Chemistry which I once attended. But if I had learnt to cook it would have been very useful had I been in any difficulty when the servants were unable to do it'. Indeed, the Housecraft Certificate remained a prominent part of the school's curriculum until 1941, when it is no longer recorded in the school magazine examination results.

1956 Home Economics class in what is now the cloakroom

Although Miss Trenerry built up a surplus of £2,500 during the First World War, staff salaries were kept at a low rate and there was a high staff turnover (possibly exacerbated by the war-time situation). The examination results of 1919 showed that only two girls gained 3rd Class Honours in the public examinations, and nearly a third of the 311 examination papers were assessed as 'bad', with a high failure rate. Miss Trenerry resigned in 1920 on her engagement to a local clergyman. Feelings about Miss Trenerry were clearly mixed. Petronella Snowball, a Sixth Former at the time and then Head Girl, recalled in later years: 'I think it is perhaps as well that the record of the Board of Education Inspection which preceded Miss Trenerry's resignation was lost. One of her perks was school dinners. I did not have them for long and I did not at all mind the black artichokes from the school garden served on uncleaned blackboards put on trestles in the Art Room and the black handled knives, but the Inspectors did.'

Miss Clara Dixon, the fifth Head, was appointed to revive the school's morale. Under Miss Dixon the School continued to provide the breadth of curriculum, including the Domestic Science subjects. She set up the school house system in 1920, with the four that still exist today, Merchant Venturers, Smiths and Armourers, Haberdashers, Goldsmiths, and two other separate houses for the boarders – Tuckers and Weavers in the two Summerlands houses, and Cordwainers for Tregear boarders.

Achievement at the School began to pick up, and in 1921, the school's Head Girl, Amy Clogg, won a £50 scholarship for Natural Sciences at Newnham College, Cambridge. In 1922, six Sixth Formers won places at universities. This remained a standard for the next two decades – in 1939 six girls went on to university, and by

Carrots and sticks

There is occasional mention by the girls of the consequences of sub-standard work or behaviour. The Lower 4 in 1904 noted that 'Miss Aldis took all that had not been on the black list to Longdown by train.' In 1908, the Upper 4 proudly mentioned that 'Our Form has had a good record this term, as we have only had four returned lessons – no order marks', whereas, in 1916, the Lower 4 observed ruefully 'We hoped to get through this term without an order mark, but we have just had two the last week'.

On the other hand, there were the occasional surprise treats. In 1911, the coronation of George V was celebrated by a 'half-holiday' for the school. The Third form noted gleefully 'We had a nice holiday in the middle of the term because of the Coronation'.

Rather unusually, the marriages of two members of staff were celebrated in the same way in 1917 – perhaps the rigours of the war-time situation needed some compensation – 'Miss Preston-Thomas and Miss Kaye have both been married this year, and Isabel Perkin won an exhibition at St Hilda's Hall, Oxford, so the School had three more half-holidays.

We also have to thank the hard winter for several afternoons off, devoted to skating on the canal.' The half-holidays sometimes involved organised activities in the school, and the Lower 4 described Miss Preston-Thomas' wedding in their end-of-year form letter: 'Last year's form captains went to the wedding, and in the afternoon we had a half-holiday, which was occupied by a junior and senior paper chase, which we enjoyed very much'. 1917 was a very notable year, with one pupil also being awarded a public scholarship: 'May Draper was successful in winning a scholarship (to Westfield College, London) and we were given a half-holiday in her honour, and we celebrated the day with sports'.

1956, 11 pupils were accepted at universities, and the school's academic progress was commended by the school's inspectors on their first visit since 1937. The curriculum and extra-curricular activity continued to expand after 1935 with the arrival of Miss Ryan as Headmistress, and 1937 saw the first school trip abroad to Bayeux and Arromanches.

The redoubtable Miss Ryan, Headmistress 1935–1962

Under Miss Ryan, in 1950–51 there was the transfer from the Cambridge Local and Higher School Certificates to a new system of O-levels and A-levels. This continues today, although since 1987 the O-levels have been called GCSEs (General Certificate of Secondary Education). Freda Jackson remembers very clearly the Maynard ethos at this time concerning examinations: 'School exams were held in the spring and summer terms. Individual teachers were not permitted to tell us our actual exam mark when returning and discussing exam papers. Instead Miss Ryan would come, unannounced, into a lesson, and read out the complete set of exam results for our class, and comment favourably or otherwise, on the performance of various girls. It certainly made the point that exams were considered important!'

By the time Gill Newport was a pupil, in the 1960s, Miss Bradley had taken over the running of the School. Gill recalls that lessons were formal and mostly 'chalk and talk', and that all pupils were expected to stand up and greet the teacher when she entered the room. Pupils were also expected to stand up if the Headmistress came into the lesson.

By the time Miss Murdin arrived in 1980 the curriculum within School was more exclusively aimed at performing in the academic sphere as opposed to domestic studies, although Textiles and Home Economics were still taught. In the 1990s the introduction of computers added ICT to the already extensive list of subjects to be studied. The choice of examination subjects was left to the candidates, in consultation with their teachers and parents. An equally extensive list of extra-curricular activities had also developed. These ranged from societies attended in school time, such as choirs, Christian Union, and science clubs, to the Duke of Edinburgh Award scheme, Ten Tors and Young Enterprise outside School.

Even as late as the 1990s the lessons still retained some of the formality noted in the 1960s, as they began with standing and greeting teachers when they entered and assembly was still taken by the Head in her academic gown. Lessons had, however, changed in style. Although there was still formal teaching many lessons now involved the pupils to a greater extent through group work, presentations and work sheets. The Maynard was certainly brimming with opportunity for girls to achieve in many different ways and this continues to the present day with a full range of activities offered to pupils.

Stained glass window in the School Hall (photo courtesy Robin Jones)

On the steps of the Palais de Justice, Rennes, 1969

U14 National Netball Finalists (National Champions), 2002

The Owl & the Pussycat at the Barnfield Theatre, c1983 (Upper 4 and Lower 5)

Upper 3 baking cakes, 2001

Newly-married Mr and Mrs Horton, August 1990, leaving Exeter Cathedral via Upper 3N's floral arch

Summer Term.

	MONDAY	TUESDAY	WEDNESDAY	THURSDAY	FRIDAY
9.15	Science.	Games	Gym	Latin	French
9.55	English.	Music	Geometry	French	Gym
10.35	Algebra.	History	Latin	History	Geometry
11.30	French.	Writing	Geography.	Science	Needlework
12.10	Latin.	Arithmetic	Scripture.	Science	
	AFTERNOON				
2.20	Art.	English	French	Games	English
3.0	Art	Latin	Algebra		Geography
	HOMEWORK				
	MONDAY	TUESDAY	WEDNESDAY	THURSDAY	FRIDAY
	English. Geography.	History Latin	Scripture Mathematics	English French	Mathematics Science

In 1941 Lower 4's form teacher set them a holiday task to make a colourful noticeboard timetable, house points being awarded for the girls' efforts. This was Mary Stark's (Haberdasher) timetable

Three fairies in the Upper 5 pantomime, 2001

'Life after School' day, 2002 – members of Lower 6 having fun team building

School trip to Spain, 2007

Lower 1 hard at work, 1983

Maynard Hockey Team at Crystal Palace, 1989

1978 Leavers' Reunion in 1998. Front row centre left: Headmistress Miss Murdin; centre right: Miss Bradley, her predecessor
(photo © Nicholas Toyne)

Head Girls' Dinner in Main School Hall, March 2006

Becci Gosling, Upper Sixth 2008, holding a genuine red shoe bag

In the School hall waiting to enter the Miss Maynard competition, 1988

The Blue Boy statue presented to the School in 1996

Mr Crew conducting the School Choir at Prize Giving 2005 (photo © Nicholas Toyne)

Comic Relief Day 2005

Upper 5 Geography field trip, 2005

Mr Collins demonstrating exciting scientific principles at Open Evening, 2006

Junior production of *Germs*, 2002
(photo © Quay Studios)

Work Experience at Exeter Cathedral Archive, 2006

Pring under construction, 1990

Drama workshop, Stratford trip 2008

Making cakes to raise funds during Red Nose Day, 2003

West U14 Girls' National Schools' Final, 2003

Training for Ten Tors with Mr and Mrs Saunders, 2008

Wartime

THE FIRST WORLD WAR (1914–1918) had some impact on the school, when everyone felt an obligation to contribute to the war effort. Many girls were involved in land work at weekends and during holidays. The annual Speech Day included an address from the local organiser: 'Miss Calmady Hamlin addressed the School at the end of the Christmas Term on behalf of the Devonshire Womens' Agricultural Committee and enrolled a great many recruits for land work. She had previously spoken at a meeting held in the School Hall on 8th December, on the work of educated women on the land. The land-working activities of the School have been chiefly confined to pulling mangold-wurzels and swedes, preparing gardens for potatoes, gardening at the Officers' Hospital at Streatham Hall, and apple-picking (at Mrs Taylor's farm, Newton St Cyres); large parties of girls worked in these different ways on most of the Saturdays last year and are still going on this Term. Working parties have been held on alternate Fridays, and we have found many small ways of being useful, such as painting the covers of the Magazine of No. 2 Hospital and picking over the sphagnum moss for surgical dressings'.

Another contribution made by the School was entertaining the wounded soldiers recovering at the handful of Exeter hospitals involved in treating war casualties. In 1917, 1918 and just after Peace Day in 1919, the School hosted a party for about 100 walking wounded from the local hospitals, which took the form of tea and a concert in the School Hall. In 1917, girls and staff presented 'a variety entertainment, including dances, coon songs, selections from Gilbert and Sullivan's Operas, sung in costume, and recitations and scenes from *Alice in Wonderland*'. In the following year, 'as well as more recitations from *Alice in Wonderland*, they had *The Pied Piper of Hamlin*. The Rats in the latter, who were allowed to run about through the audience, provided a source of intense amusement to our guests'.

Maynardian rats in the 1918 production of *Pied Piper of Hamelin*

The Second World War (1939–1945) had an immense impact on the School when in May 1942 not only was Exeter badly bombed but the Maynard was hit. Tregear, Junior school and the main building were all damaged by the blast, and one girl was killed, albeit not on school premises. In 1940, the School had taken 30 schoolgirl evacuees from London (from St Paul's, Haberdashers, and Ashford School), onto the school roll for a few months and in 1942, after the bombing, it was the turn of Maynard girls to accept guest accommodation at Hele's, Bishop Blackall and Exeter Schools, while the School was out of action. The neighbouring private house, Leebourne, housed two families. Their respective daughters, Ann Sant and Fay Beecham were Maynard pupils, both about eight years old. Leebourne was hit in the raid and, tragically, Fay was killed. It was thought that she and a disabled relative had remained in the house while the rest of the families went to the shelter. Leebourne was later sold to the School and became the site of the new Sports Hall. Summerlands boarding house was destroyed in the bombing, the boarders having been safely evacuated beforehand, but by the end of May alternative accommodation had been arranged at Rixlade, Stoke Hill, north of Exeter. School repairs were financed in the post-war years by the Government's War Damage repair fund, a grant from the Ministry of Education, and a small amount of extra funding from the St John's Hospital Trust. The stained glass window in the school hall was very badly damaged, but when it came to be replaced some years later the stained glass firm which had originally built the window was able to supply an exact reproduction using the templates and drawings it had retained since the construction of the first window in 1883.

Rixlade, the bombed-out boarders' temporary accommodation

Audrey Jones remembers that with the wartime shortage of paper every line on a page had to be used before a new book could be issued. 'At one stage we all had "printators" for scrap notes. These were reusable by withdrawing the centre board and pushing it back again. Any pointed object could be used to write on the top layer which was transparent soft Perspex or similar.'

Geography walks and field trips

MANY OF THE FORM LETTERS of the early years talk about the enjoyment of school outings into the local countryside, often with the educational theme of Geography or Geology. In 1909, the Geography mistress, Miss Williams, took some of the classes on memorable outings that were enthusiastically described in the yearly form letters in the magazine. The Lower 5 wrote: 'We have been for several geography walks with Miss Williams. The first time we took the train to Digby's Halt and walked to Clyst St. Mary and had our tea in a field there while we watched the river. On July 7th we went to the top of Pennsylvania, down Wreford Lane and by Prospect Park, and returned along the Cowley Road. On this walk we studied the different kinds of clouds, the work of weirs, and contours.' The Upper 5 had a slightly more adventurous outing in the run-up to their public exams: 'This term, just before our Higher Certificate examinations, Miss Williams took us to Chudleigh Rocks where we had an exciting afternoon. We took candles with us and explored the limestone caves'. Again in 1909 the Sixth Form enjoyed their outing with their form mistress, Miss Haslam. 'We went to Ladram Bay, and after dinner walked over the cliffs to Budleigh Salterton, where we had tea. We had a most delightful day, and gathered lovely bunches of flowers. It was most exciting trying to wash our hands in the sea.'

Much later, in the latter half of the century, the range and type of field trips being undertaken would have seemed astonishing to the earlier Maynardians. Sylvia Wickenden, Head of Geography 1966–1989, recalls: 'Geography Field Trips: for some an incentive to do the subject, for others quite the reverse. They tended to involve a lot of exercise, often in inclement weather requiring boots and waterproofs (very unglamorous), with cold hands and feet, and evenings of follow-up work in the Geography department or in Youth Hostels. In the latter some very unusual culinary concoctions often preceded the evening's work but in the former local fish and chips helped the evening along (and left the Geography room smelling of fish and chips next morning). Locally we went to Dartmoor to measure hummocks and periglacial stone stripes by Cox's Tor; we walked down the River Sid and measured stream flows – occasionally waist-deep – and we teamed up with the Biologists to squidge about on Budleigh Salt Marsh or to brave the adders on Woodbury Common (only one was actually seen). In alternate years we went to the Lake District and Tyneside, taking in the Roman Wall on the Great Whin Sill between them. On earlier trips we climbed Helvellyn and toiled up to Scales Tarn to look at glacial features, often in snow. Later, when measuring things became the 'in' thing, we studied glacial mounds in Borrowdale and at Easedale Tarn. Tyneside surprised every group. Expecting a forbidding, gloomy city, its fine architecture and bridges and (especially) the Metro and Eldon shopping centres soon changed opinions, and visits to Consett and later Teesside iron and steel works with showers of sparks as steel was poured and orange-hot steel bars trundled by on conveyor belts impressed everyone. Even studies of urban blight were offset by the imaginative Byker Wall, though New Town Peterlee left most cold – figuratively as well as literally. The friendliness of the people of Tyneside was epitomised by the Lord Mayor who invited us one year to a Civic Reception at the Mansion House. He was a kindly avuncular man who was very understanding of our boots and rather muddy trousers!'

Yorkshire 2008. Even with today's high-tech equipment Geography field trips are just as much as fun as in the past

Sport and games

GAMES AND EXERCISE, in many different forms, have long been an important part of Maynard life. The 1902 school magazine records some early sporting endeavours: 'Throughout the [spring] term Wednesday afternoon and Saturday morning were devoted to learning basket ball and rounders in the school ground [sic], under the direction of Miss Le Couteur and Miss Chambers, with the result that one rounders match and two basket ball matches were played during the term. [Summer term]: Cricket and rounders took the place of basket ball, and the School had the glory of beating an outside team, the first outside team it has ever played, which may be considered a happy augury of the future.' 1902 was also the year a Games Club was started. Tennis was first recorded in 1904 although, apparently, didn't get off to a very good start: 'The standard of play was exceedingly low, and the Games Committee would be glad to see more keenness shown for the game.' In 1906 Basket Ball [sic] matches are recorded for the first time but no mention of Tennis although by 1910 things were looking up: 'Challenging in [Form] Ties was taken up with much more vigour this year than previously, with the result that the style of play considerably improved.' By 1917 Lacrosse and Net-Ball [sic] had been added to the range of games played.

1st XI Cricket team, 1930

In the early 1900s each class also went through a 10-minute Drill routine every day, with certain pupils taking part in the annual Drill Display presented to parents and visitors in the spring term. Tregear boarder Mary Westall wrote in 1914: 'Last term we began our drilling exercises in the evening. At 8.30pm all the Boarding House except the Fifths and Sixths appeared on the landing robed in their nightgowns and dressing gowns, ready to perform their exercises. It often looked most oriental in the half-light with several people in kimonos.' The usual sports teams for Hockey, Netball, Cricket and Tennis played fixtures with other schools, sometimes with the boys at Collingwood School. This school was run by the parents of Lily Parsons, (who became Head Girl; later a Classics Mistress and who also wrote the School Song), and Lily's brothers appeared in the Collingwood Hockey and Cricket teams that played matches with the Maynard girls. Sometimes the girls won, although a report of one of these matches in the magazine noted that 'Our team did not play so well on the whole as usual. The fielding, in fact, was rather disgraceful, there being a great number of dropped catches.' Cricket was clearly very important in the life of the school. 'Another great event of the summer term was the Cricket Supper, when we had the pleasure of welcoming our victorious team back from Plymouth. We all had supper at Tregear. At the end speeches were made and thanks returned to Miss Trenerry and Miss Goodman for giving the supper and the health of the team was proposed and seconded. After supper we went over to the Hall and had dancing and games for the rest of the evening.' In 1912, the magazine began to report on the individual performances of team members, with comments such as 'P Lucas: Although a promising player, has been somewhat disappointing. Hits everything in the air, and is very uncertain'. This form of individual criticism was not repeated again save for a brief reappearance in the 1927/28 magazine within a 'Criticism of the Team' section: 'M Woodland: A useful member in the circle, but found difficulty in running straight in mid-field.'

The measles scare of 1909 affected the fixtures programme for the summer term, and school teams had to play each other with some interesting variations, as this Cricket report for that year revealed: 'All outside matches had unfortunately to be cancelled owing to illness in the school. A match was organised for the half-term holiday entitled 'Beauty v Brains'. The sides were decided by lottery, the players being thus relieved of the necessity of

School Tennis team, c1940

deciding in which direction their own particular virtue lay. The game was both amusing and exciting and resulted in a victory to the 'Brains'.'

There was no sports day until 1911: 'A new departure this year was the School Sports', and the Drill Display was the big event of the year. The games mistress was responsible for drill exercise throughout the School but there was an intriguing comment from a Lower 4 girl in 1907: 'We have not a drilling mistress now so games are taken by Sergt Busby'. Perhaps all the girls were super-fit that year, although the significant number of girls who went on to Physical Education College sometimes had fitness problems. Joyce Allen, who went on to Bedford Physical Training College in 1919 wrote to the school magazine that 'During the first week, the juniors might easily be recognised on account of "Junior Leg" – a horrible disease attacking the legs after strenuous gymnastics'. Sports Day ceased prior to the First World War and wasn't held again until 1939.

The standard of playing in all games steadily increased over the years with, during the 1950s and 60s, Hockey, Rounders and, one year, Sports Day, taking place in a field off Barrack Road until it became the site of the new Royal Devon & Exeter Hospital. From time to time new sports were added to the curriculum, for example, in 1936 the first swimming lessons were held on Saturday mornings in the King's Alley Baths. Swimming quickly became an important activity and was greatly encouraged. The 1969 magazine reports: 'The standard of the swimming in the Gala was higher than it has ever been, and five school records were broken.' 1973 was particularly noteworthy in this respect: 'The highlight of this past year has been the use we have had of the re-conditioned, heated open-air bath at Exeter School … We can be proud of the fact that there is no one in the Main School, and there are only a few children in Traceyville, who cannot now swim.' In 1972 Mrs Underhill started an Athletics Club, for which the girls went to the Clifton Hill track, and there was also a thriving Fencing Club. The Athletics group was flourishing in 1973 but, unfortunately, the School lost its Fencing coach, although two Sixth Formers continued working with the younger girls to maintain enthusiasm in this sport. Athletics must have fallen by the wayside at some point as the 1983 school magazine notes: 'In the summer, we introduced athletics for the first time for several years.'

Sports Day, 1961

The following year, however, marked a real turning in the sporting life and facilities at the school: 'The season 1984–85 must surely be one of the most memorable in the sporting history of the Maynard School. The highlights of the year were the completion of Bradley Hall in March 1985 and reaching the finals of both the U16 Barclays Bank National Hockey Championship and the U18 Mercian Indoor Hockey Championship … the first time we have reached a national final in any sport except tennis … to manage this twice in one season in two different aged groups is an outstanding achievement. Already Bradley Hall has proved invaluable and is so versatile.' It is notable that the Sport Report in the school magazine had by now grown to eight pages rather than the two or three of earlier years, reflecting its growth in importance in Maynard life. This was further reinforced in 1994 when A-level Physical Education was added to the curriculum 'to provide an opportunity for studying this increasingly popular subject.'

Of the extra-curricular sporting activities a particular high spot was an equestrian one in 1992 when three Lower Sixth girls represented the Maynard at the Senior Schools Championship at Hickstead in Sussex. Out of over 70 teams the Maynard team came seventh which was a fantastic achievement. This sort of activity, together with things like the Netball tour to Barbados in 1996, would have seemed incredible to those early girls taking part in the school's first outside match back in 1902.

The Maynard Old Girls

MISS PURDIE SET UP THE MAYNARD SCHOOL OLD GIRLS' SOCIETY (MSOGS) when she arrived as Headmistress in 1902. The school magazine of that year records: 'A very great event at the beginning of the summer term was the Inaugural Meeting of the Old Girls' Society, which was made all the greater by a visit from Miss Hall, the first headmistress of the school'.

There were, of course, the reunion evenings held at the School two or three times a year for fun and enjoyment, but a large part of the activities supported by the Old Girls who still lived in Exeter involved charitable work in the community.

A big commitment was running the weekly youth clubs for girls (and later a separate club for boys). These were called the Children's Happy Evenings. At the end of each autumn term there was always a party which included presentation of Christmas gifts. The 1904 magazine reported that 'Money and labour was raised to present each child with a red serge petticoat – given away by the Mayoress, Mrs F W Widgery, at Christmas'.

After four years, in 1907, the club moved from the Market Hall to new and more comfortable premises at St Mary Arches Street School, loaned at no charge by the Governors of that school. The reports show no awareness of the fact that this was next door to the site where the original Maynard School, the Blue Maids' Hospital, functioned for over 200 years.

'Old Maynardians v The School' Tennis match at the summer meeting, June 1928

The Old Girls branched out to set up a separate Happy Evening for boys. The organiser, Hilda McCrea, described her turn to help run the evening. 'We began work in the Market Hall on January 22nd with the names of four helpers on our books and twelve little Central School boys, as we were not at all sure what effect the Happy Evenings would have on them, or how we should be able to manage them; we soon found that they gave little or no trouble. If any Old Girls can spare one hour a week to come and help us with our little boys, she would find that though they are ragged and sometimes far from clean, they are very entertaining and easy to work with. Some of the children have a keen sense of humour, as I once experienced when sitting between two of them, who, I am sorry to say, had started quarrelling while at their basket work. I did not at first interfere, but when A accused B of being a "liard", and B said he would "bash" A's nose for him, I interposed with a "Hush, hush", upon which B looked at me with a little smile and remarked "'Ushed was the evenin' 'ymn", and peace reigned once more'.

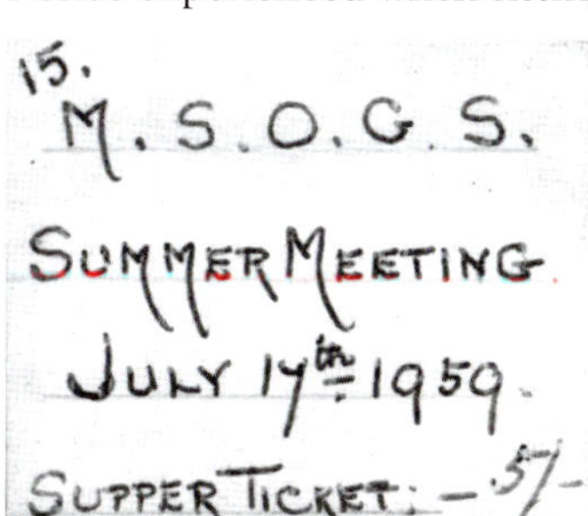

Nothing was wasted in those days – carefully hand-written supper ticket cut from the corner of a postcard

Finding enough volunteer helpers was a constant problem, especially during the war years, and in 1917 the secretary's report took on a reproachful tone. 'Work had to be carried on in a very small way owing to the lack of helpers. The Head and Secretary were the only two helpers left, and if the Misses Carr had not come to the rescue, the work could not have been carried on at all … As it was, the Tinies could never do any work, and very often the big girls had to play on their work nights [they were supposed to alternate 'work' and 'play' evenings each week]. On the last night of the autumn term, every child was given a little Christmas present and an orange, as treats [the usual Party] are now a thing of the past. We are very badly in want of some more helpers in order that the evenings may be carried on in a proper way, as naturally the children get a bit out of hand with so few to look after them.' The last report came in 1919: 'Sad to say that the Children's Happy Evenings were shut down in December owing to the Secretary leaving Exeter, and no one being found to carry on the work; this was a great blow to her as she had worked at the club right from its opening night, October 22nd 1903. It seemed extraordinary that amongst all the Old Girls, no one could be found to carry on this happy work. (E P Marsh. Hon Sec).' Perhaps all the Exeter Old Girls reading this report felt suitably chastened.

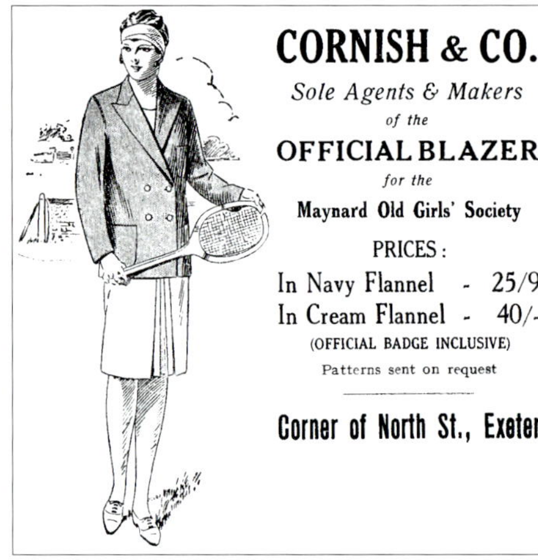

For many years the Old Girls' Society had its own 'uniform'. In 1924 they passed a resolution that they would have blazers. However, it seems that there was some difficulty in deciding on a colour so they compromised by agreeing to have two – navy flannel for winter and cream flannel for summer. Both had a badge on the pocket embroidered in silver thread, and three silver buttons on each sleeve. In 1931 they introduced their own 'school' tie – navy blue background with two light blue stripes, edged with narrow white stripes and a narrow scarlet stripe through the middle.

Jeanne Watkins (later Shattock), back row 4th from right, Lower 5 1945. In the centre is Miss Baker, Domestic Science and Form Teacher.

The MSOGS was an extremely active society for many decades, with a full programme of events and regional meetings every year. For many years they mounted their own drama productions on a fairly regular basis. In 1906 the OGA Dramatic Club Report states 'It was also decided that some play should be given at the Holiday meeting in January, and a Sub-Committee decided that the members should work at two scenes from *Cranford*. … these, and a scene from *The Rivals*, were enjoyed by an enthusiastic audience.' Sheridan must have been a popular playwright during the early 1900s as *The Rivals* was performed yet again, along with a 'Shakespearian Recital', in 1911. In 1907 the Old Girls undertook a production of *Pygmalion* along with *Galatea* at the Christmas Holiday meeting.

In 1978 it was decided to try and trace any Maynard Old Boys. Out of 10 contacted, four wished to join the Society so, in 1979, MSOGS was renamed the Old Maynardians' Society (OMS). In the same year, due to falling numbers, it was decided also to close down the London Branch of the Society.

In October 1984 everyone was stunned by the death of the OMs Chairman, Mrs Jeanne Shattock, in the IRA bomb attack on the Grand Hotel, Brighton. Her involvement with, and commitment to the Maynard had spanned many years: as Jeanne Watkins she had been a pupil from 1942–1947; her daughter Clare was a pupil from 1966–1976, and in 1977 Jeanne had become a School Governor followed by Chairman of OMS in 1979. Her untimely and tragic death was a great loss to both the School and the wider community that she served in many different ways, as well as to her family. As if to compound the awfulness of that year, the Society was dismayed to hear that it was running at a loss and urgent action was needed to rectify this. It took three years for this situation to improve.

From 1993 onwards the Old Maynardians' Society published its own separate magazine and the Old Maynardians' section ceased to appear in the school magazine. The OMS also adopted the Maynard '3 hands' crest as their logo prior to the current 'M' school logo being brought in during 1997 in place of the crest.

OMS continues to flourish and to be an important part of Maynard life, both by the annual donation that the Society makes to the Head's discretionary fund and the interest and involvement Old Maynardians maintain on a practical level. The 350th celebrations have proved a wonderful opportunity to work even more closely with the Old Maynardians and to re-establish contact with many who were 'lost'.

The Maynard enters the 21st century

Dr Daphne West
(Headmistress 2000–2008)

IT IS AN IMPRESSIVELY SOBERING THOUGHT that, although 'only' 350 years old, the Maynard's history now spans five centuries, from the 17th to the 21st. My period as Headmistress of the Maynard began on 1st January 2000 – a suitably symbolic date – and the beginning of the fifth century in which the Maynard has been part of the lives of *filiae Devonienses*. Clearly, the life of the School and the job of the Headmistress have changed radically over time; whilst some essential features and qualities of the School's life remain the same from decade to decade, other changes have been dramatic and rapid.

My predecessors established some impressive principles in terms of the ethos of the School: that initiative, originality, ingenuity and tenacity should be valued and encouraged, that no two girls are ever the same, that individual strengths should be fostered, and weaknesses strengthened, and that everyone needs to learn to cope with disappointment, as well as success. The Maynard certainly knew about, and practised, 'individualised learning' long before a 21st-century Minister of Education came up with the phrase.

Initiative, originality, ingenuity and tenacity should be valued and encouraged, individual strengths should be fostered, and weaknesses strengthened...

In January 2000 the Maynard was faced with a particular problem: how to continue its selective intake, its wide-ranging curriculum and its programme of fees assistance in the face of the withdrawal of the Government's Assisted Places Scheme, which in January 2000 was still funding almost a third of the pupils in the School. A huge role in ensuring that the Maynard was able to maintain its pupil numbers and its curriculum has been played by its astonishingly active and committed 21st-century Governing Body. The Chairmen of Governors during my headship – Professor Mark MacNair, Mr Robin Thomas and Mrs Topsy Murray – have shown quite remarkable wisdom and tenacity in their support of the School. The Maynard is unusual in the composition of its Governing Body (with elected Parent and Staff Governors), and also in its Bursar, Tom Hughes-Parry, whose long service to the School (since 1981), formidable accounting skills, knowledge of charity law and absolute commitment to the welfare of the Maynard's pupils have played a key part in the School's continuing success.

My two immediate predecessors, Joan Bradley and Felicity Murdin, were both incredibly kind and helpful to me in my first years in post. It was a privilege to be part of the Cathedral service in 2001 commemorating Miss Bradley's life; her brain and her wit were both razor-sharp even in her final years, and her memory phenomenal. I recall Miss Bradley describing how she constructed the academic timetable: on the floor of the Main School Hall, with various pieces of paper which she moved around with her feet until she got it sorted. Not for her the board with magnetic attachments, nor the complex computer software of 2008. Miss Murdin has kept close links with the School since her retirement in 1999, and we were all delighted that in January 2004 she was able to be the Guest of Honour who opened the refurbished Ryan House, with its new Sixth Form accommodation and the very special English Room dedicated to the memory of Rosemary Langley, our much-loved Head of English, who lost her brave battle against cancer in 2002. In our 350th year, Miss Murdin performed her second opening ceremony, when the Murdin Link was opened – a two-storey, five-classroom building to replace the Hauser building (variously a home for Biology and Geography), a sturdy 'temporary structure' erected not long after the Second World War damage to the site.

I will name just two of the more striking management challenges posed during my eight years at the helm: babies and ICT. I am sure the collective eyebrows of some of my predecessors would shoot up by a matter of inches at the information that in my eight years and one month in post there were 50 maternity and paternity leaves amongst our teaching and non-teaching staff. I have strong recollections of a dream (or was it a nightmare?) I had in 2003, when each member of staff, male and female, from the novice teacher through to senior colleagues nearing retirement, were all queuing outside my office to explain when their baby was due! When I joined the Maynard, Mrs Boyce and Mrs MacBryde had already shown visionary leadership in establishing the foundations of Information and Communications Technology. ICT is certainly a strong competitor for the title of biggest spender in the School's budget – developments are so swift that new hardware is more or less out of date by the time it is unpacked from its box. ICT has also increased the expectations of parents, pupils and colleagues that requests, complaints, congratulations and information will all be dealt with instantaneously by e-mail. The Maynard has been fortunate indeed to have so many knowledgeable and committed staff to guide the School through the information revolution. And it is true that technology has changed many of the Maynard's ways in the first decade of the 21st century: from hand-written reports in shoe-boxes to a fully integrated database; from overhead transparencies to instant internet access in the classroom, to name but two.

One of the great things about headship is the sheer variety of what one has to deal with, in both academic and human terms. It was certainly a challenge for both staff and pupils to introduce and manage the AS and A2 system: suddenly there was no longer a whole Lower Sixth year to delve into a subject – just two terms, effectively, of teaching and learning before the AS exams struck early in the summer term. There were compensations, though, in the opportunity to retake 'units' in each subject.

Events on a national level can have a huge impact on the life of a school, and in the first decade of the 21st century the Maynard faced significant non-academic challenges. A petrol shortage in 2001 created by striking tanker drivers (which at least encouraged parents to share the delivery of pupils to school each day), led one parent to ask me 'what I was going to do about the shortage of petrol' (I rather thought that was Tony Blair's job!). The dreadful Foot and Mouth outbreak of 2001 affected the whole school community, with some particularly sad individual cases of girls living on farms where hundreds of animals were slaughtered. During this particular crisis, Mrs Martin inspired the school community to raise money to help affected farmers by sponsoring girls and staff to dress up as farmers for the day. I borrowed a flat cap and a checked shirt, and duly clad in wellingtons, I arrived at school with many other 'Farmer Giles' look-alikes, completely forgetting that the Headmistress of St Margaret's at the time, Mrs Maureen D'Albertanson, had been invited to lunch: we clearly convinced her of the Maynard's capacity for eccentricity!

The Maynard's site is tightly packed with buildings, and yet we retain some very pleasant green areas. The newest of these areas is the Garden of Reflection, a haven of tranquillity in the busy lives of all Maynardians, constructed in the aftermath of the Ufton Nervet train crash in November 2004, in which Maynardian Emily Webster was killed, and three other Maynardians injured, including myself. The train crash was an episode in the School's history which demonstrated time and again that mutual support is an outstanding feature of the Maynard community.

Mrs Boyce (2nd row, 3rd from right) with colleagues and pupils in the 1975 School photo

The Maynard has been fortunate indeed in recruiting the highest calibre of teaching and non-teaching staff over the years, and to have benefited from their striking loyalty and long service. Many girls and staff, for example, owe a singular debt of gratitude to Mrs Ann Boyce, who celebrates 35 years of service to the Maynard in its 350th year.

The most salient feature of the Maynard remains the inspirational talent and energy of its pupils: girls regularly gain national recognition in sport and music, excel in all sorts of professions and undertake everything from launching a charity with street children in Peru to opening an orphanage in Uganda, not to mention saving turtles in Costa Rica, or combining a legal career with working as a volunteer lumberjack in Canada. Many Old Maynardians have talked to me about how Maynard experiences have shaped their lives – for example: 'I think that the Maynard gave me a fantastic start in life – not just in terms of exam grades, but also learning various tedious sounding things like discipline and self-reliance, that actually seem to get you further than you'd imagine'.

Planning for the School's 350th anniversary, and for the establishment of the 350th Foundation, has involved many current and former staff and pupils. 'Education is what survives when what has been learned has been forgotten' (B F Skinner in the *New Scientist*, 1964) was a quotation very much brought to mind on 31st March 2006, when we welcomed back to school 36 former Head Girls for a dinner to launch our 350th Anniversary plans. As we made arrangements for this event, we wondered how easy it would be to cater for guests who ranged in age from 18 to over 80. We need not have worried. The sense of energetic interest was palpable, as octogenarians and their younger counterparts shared their Maynardian experiences and spoke of their lives and careers. The opportunity to listen to those who had been chosen as Maynard leaders over a 60-year period confirmed that there is, indeed, 'something about the Maynard': there was a sense that all these generations of women truly valued their education and had left the Maynard with the confidence to leave their 'comfort zones' and to seize opportunities to make a difference to society in a whole range of careers in this country and all over the world. One former Head Girl told me that one of the best things she had acquired as part of her Maynard education was the capacity to be constantly intrigued by things – she recalled the words of Eleanor Roosevelt: 'One thing life has taught me: if you are interested, you never have to look for new interests. They come to you. When you are genuinely interested in one thing, it will always lead to something else.'

I often wonder what Sir John Maynard would have made of the Maynard today – he would surely have been surprised at the range of the pupils' experience, and, I hope, have felt a sense of pleasure for the girls and pride in their achievements. Interestingly, the most common career path chosen by former Maynardians (for whom we have information) is in education, including an Oxford professor, and an assistant professor of History at a US university. The second most significant group is composed of Maynardian medics; there are at least five consultants practising in Devon alone. Old Maynardians feature prominently in the world of Veterinary Medicine and the Law, whilst the business arena has our former students working at senior leadership and executive levels with top international companies. Amongst exciting job titles we have a Political Risk Analyst, a Forensic Researcher, and a Technical Translator for Patents. In the Arts, we have professional musicians and dancers performing internationally, and a poet, as well as a Booker Prize-nominated author. Former students are working for the BBC, and we have an editor at the Oxford University Press, a librarian at the Bodleian, a Curator of Children's Literature at Frederick Warne, and a curator at the Victoria & Albert Museum. A significant number of Maynardians are self-employed in a range of careers from business consultancy to bookselling, with many working in the voluntary sector. In other words, whatever professional circles you move in, you are almost bound to bump into a Maynardian.

Dr West and her two labradors, Hector and Ollie, with one of the 2008 Ten Tors teams: Alicia Caunter, Holly Gillard, Emma Rogers, Alicia Thew, Sophie Palmer and Izzy Hayes.

My period as Headmistress of the Maynard ends in December 2008 – what a privilege to have been part of this magnificent educational establishment!

From School Magazine 1963-64

"Sheila Tremaine is home on leave. Since 1958 she has been living with an Indian tribe, the Aripaksta, a thousand miles up the Amazon. The Aripaksta saw white men for the first time only four years ago, and their customs and living conditions, which Sheila shares, are extremely primitive. In spite of the risks and enormous difficulties involved in teaching them the ways of civilisation, Sheila hopes to be able to stay long enough to learn their language, with a view to producing a translation of the New Testament for them."

Development of the Maynard School buildings

Mary Ellis
(Pupil 1958–1972; teacher of Physics 1990–2003; Senior Academic Administrator 2003–current)

A VISITOR APPROACHING FROM BARNFIELD ROAD now sees only a bank of trees, but originally the fine red-brick frontage would have created an impressive first view of the School. For many years, the central entrance was not in use, but in 1998 a reception area was created there by absorbing the room at the foot of the stairs which had variously been the prefects' room and a staff work room.

Main School building 1925

Turning left out of Reception, the visitor might be surprised to find that the cloakroom, known to generations since 1911 as 'King's Cross', has disappeared and been replaced by a dining centre with a spectacular transparent curved roof, created in 1992–93. The cloakroom is now on the left, although changing for PE lessons takes place in the sports hall or gym changing areas. There is no longer any need for shoe-holes: the only clothing left here is the girls' PE kit, stored in kit bags in large pigeonholes. (For a few years every girl had a metal locker in the cloakroom, but keeping track of the keys became too much of a headache! Now there are lockers in form rooms for girls' valuables and books.) This area, together with the adjoining Reprographics Room, has had various different uses, most recently a Chemistry laboratory, and previously for Cookery.

1955/56 A-level Chemistry class in what is now the Kitchen

At the north-eastern corner of the building a staff dining area has replaced a Sixth Form science teaching room; previously this was a Sixth Form cloakroom, in what had once been the Kindergarten room, then the 'Crafts Room', and for a while the Music Room. Adjoining that, the Chef Manager's office is where the Science technician worked when the current kitchens were the General Science laboratory. Previous generations would have known that as a Cookery room or, before 1938, the Library. Beyond this is the 1894 foundation stone for the 'Laboratory and Cookery School', initially a separate building and one of the first additions to the original school. The corner room became the Physics laboratory with the other being used for Biology by 1924, but in 1958 they were combined to create a large Physics laboratory when Biology moved out to its own building in the middle of the site. In 1991 it was completely re-fitted for Drama. A mezzanine room created above the Upper 5 cloakroom in 1984 provides a staff room for the English Department, affectionately known as 'the boudoir'.

Exiting the Reception area into the main corridor, you pass a door on your left commonly known as the 'stoke hole' door, dating from when the caretaker's job was a live-in appointment tending the coal-fired boiler.

Back in the main corridor, further along on the left, are two small rooms, now offices for the Bursar and the Senior Academic Administrator. Many generations knew these as the PE store and the 'rems' (remedial) room, the latter being both the venue for eye tests and also bunk beds for when one felt ill. More recently, the smaller room was the photocopying room and the larger the Domestic Bursar's office. Opposite these are the Headmistress's study and the School Office, although most Old Maynardians will remember these as the staff rooms, with pigeonholes outside for handing in work. At the end of this corridor is a sunny room, originally the Headmistress' sitting room. Having been a classroom and then the staff dining room, this now accommodates the Bursary staff. Incredibly, until 2004 they were based elsewhere in the city.

This corner of the building, originally built as accommodation for the Headmistress, is three storeys high. At the top now are two classrooms and a tiny staircase leading to the space under the roof and a long steep fire-escape (which has only had proper steps since 1955, when the 'ladder' was replaced). The Classics Department uses this space, with the Second-hand Uniform shop beyond it. That had been a book store until Governors became worried that the joists were not strong enough to support the weight, and

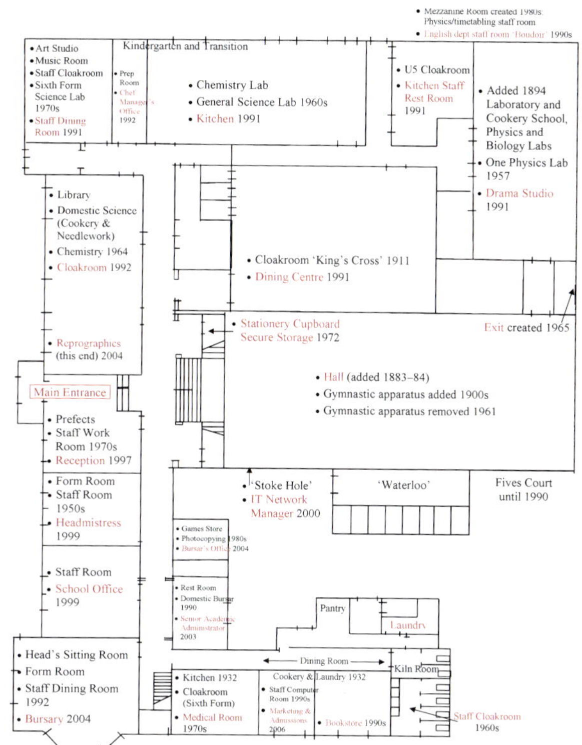

Main School: Ground Floor

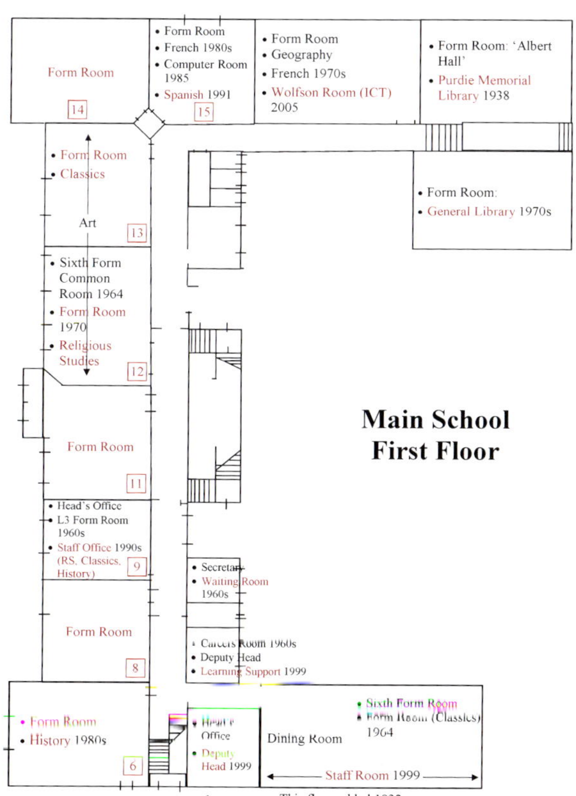

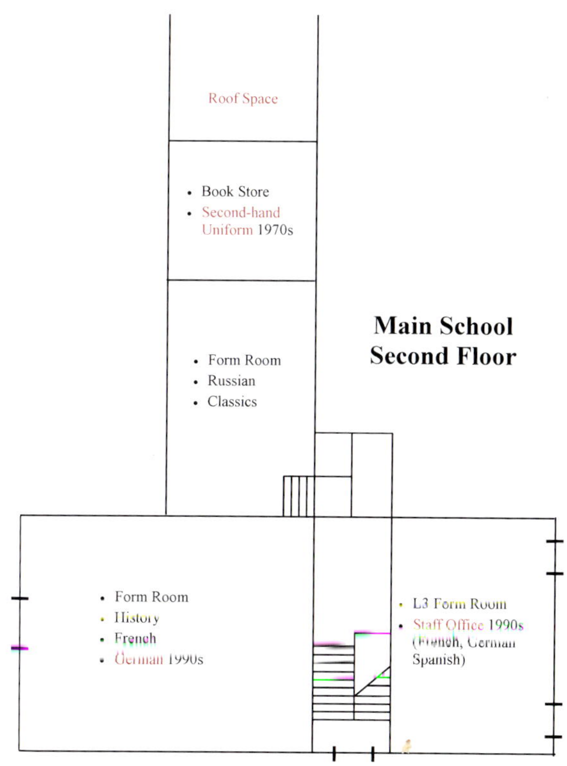

Floor plans of Main School building indicating changes and approximate dates. Today's room numbers and uses are shown in red.

had the books moved downstairs. The roof space beyond contains the giant ducts which provide fresh air to the rooms on the top corridor, drawn in through the 'cupola' on the roof and distributed via grilles in the ceilings. The small class room on the top landing is now used by Modern Languages staff; in the 1960s it had been used by Lower 3, as their forms were smaller in size than most, with the other Lower 3 being in Room 9 on the first floor – also now a staff area, for the History, Religious Studies and Classics departments. Lower 3 later had form rooms in Tregear, and then moved to Traceyville (Junior School), but now are in the new Murdin Link. There were two forms in each year group from Lower 3 upwards for many years: these were considered to be parallel, so one was named Lower 3 (L3) and the other L3P (P for parallel). Girls would generally stay in the same groups, but with different form teachers each year. In the heyday of the Government's Assisted Places Scheme, the School expanded to three forms per year from Upper 3 upwards, and these were then named U3N, U3P and U3Q, much to the confusion of new staff and girls!

1963 Lower Sixth sitting on fire escape

The southern wing was initially a single storey which housed the Kindergarten, later the Art room, and the school kitchen. In 1932 an additional storey was added, creating a new dining room, though girls also ate in the Hall when necessary; the old dining area on the ground floor was converted for Cookery and a laundry. Latterly it was divided into the book store, the Marketing & Admissions office (previously a staff computer room) and the Medical room. The upper floor later provided the Head's study and the school office, with a form room at the far end distinguished by steps up to a fire escape through the window: this was for a while used by Sixth Form girls. In 1999 this was all re-modelled to make one large staff room, with the Deputy Head taking over the Head's office.

In the centre of the building is the Assembly Hall, where gymnastics equipment was added by 1907 (previously gymnastics had been taught in the cloakroom), providing the only opportunity for exercise on wet days: the holes in the floor to which the wall bars were anchored are still clear to see. On the first floor towards the north end are two rooms (now called 12 and 13) which had long been one large room divided only by a partition. This had been the Art room, and in 1964 became a Sixth Form base. One half was their common room, with the other used for teaching; staff banged the partition when necessary to obtain relative quiet from those 'working' next door. Around the corner is the large classroom looking out over the tennis court. This was the home of the Geography department for many years, with specially-designed desks constructed in pairs to create a flat surface for maps. After a period as a French teaching room, in 2005 it was turned into a second IT room. Up a few steps beyond this, the large room on the left (affectionately known as the Albert Hall), was converted to the Purdie Memorial Library in 1938. On the right is the 'General Library', created from a form room in 1974 with funding from that year's Summer Fete. In 2003 the Librarian's desk was moved there and a barcode system of issuing books installed, with associated detectors across the doorway.

The Junior Department (which from about 1902 until 1949 included boys in the youngest years) gained its own building in 1923 when the house called Traceyville became available, along with land enough to create two tennis courts. It accommodated five classrooms, cloakroom space and staff facilities, and three music rooms which became the hub of the Music department from 1954 onwards. In 1938 the building was enlarged with the addition of its Hall and two classrooms above it, long used by Lower 1 and Form 2. An additional room was built on its south side in the 1960s.

In 1912 the school had bought Tregear, the house on the Spicer Road corner, together with some garden and a tennis court, for use as a boarding house. Matron's drawing room overlooked the entrance, although girls returning clandestinely could avoid detection by going the 'long way round' from the gate to the front door! When Tregear ceased to be used for boarders, Art, Music and Domestic Science moved in (with Needlework on the ground floor and Cookery at the top). Then Home Economics moved out to its own block (vacated by Biology) in the 1990s, leaving only Music and Art.

Across the drive is the Sixth Form building, erected in 1970. The teaching rooms upstairs could both be divided by partitions to give a space for silent work adjoining the lesson. This arrangement did not last long: one room was permanently divided to leave a small teaching room and an office for the Head of Sixth Form. A study/resources area was later added on the ground floor, accessed from the Gym changing room. An extensive development in 2003 filled in the space between Ryan House and the Gym, creating a study room equipped with computers and Careers and Further Education information, and two more large teaching rooms.

The centre of the present site is occupied by the large three-storey building called after a Chairman of the Governors, Herman Pring. This space had been occupied only by bicycle sheds until a single-story dining centre and kitchen was erected there in 1954. This survived until 1990, when it made way for the Maths and Science facilities. During this project there were no kitchens in the School so everyone ate packed lunches in their form rooms. However, the end result was worth the sacrifice, with six new large laboratories along with smaller teaching, preparation and staff rooms. On the ground floor the teaching rooms are dedicated to Mathematics, doubling as desirable form rooms for the Upper Fifths. There is also a purpose-built computer room (replacing the inadequate facilities in the upstairs corner room in the Main School), and a room initially dedicated to Design Technology. The latter did not continue in the curriculum for long, and that room has since been used by Biology and then the Mathematics department.

As ever throughout its history, the Maynard is doing its best to squeeze its quart into the pint-pot-sized site which it owns.

Outside there is very little space for Physical Education. Currently there is a double tennis court (Tregear Courts) and one single court (Bottom Court). A fives court had been created in the early years at one side of the Hall, but that was sacrificed in the construction of the Pring building; the Gymnasium was erected in 1958, in time to celebrate the 300th anniversary of the founding of the school. Leebourne, the grassed area between Spicer Road and Barnfield Hill, is barely large enough for Rounders, particularly since a temporary classroom was erected in 2003. Alongside Spicer Road there had been another tennis court (Top Court), and a row of small, brick-edged gardens where junior girls learnt gardening skills. These were lost when Bradley Hall was created in 1984, after much debate about how and where it should be placed. It had to be sunk below ground level to appease the planners, but has been invaluable to the school, as well as providing space for many city clubs in the evenings.

To celebrate the 350th anniversary, a tricky building project has replaced the two Geography rooms (originally the Biology laboratory) with the Murdin Link, providing five classrooms and physically linked to the Home Economics department, the Junior Department, and the Library in the main school building. The second phase of this project, scheduled for 2009/10, will re-model the Junior department to give better facilities, with a larger Hall and improved Library. As ever throughout its history, the Maynard is doing its best to squeeze its quart into the pint-pot-sized site which it owns.

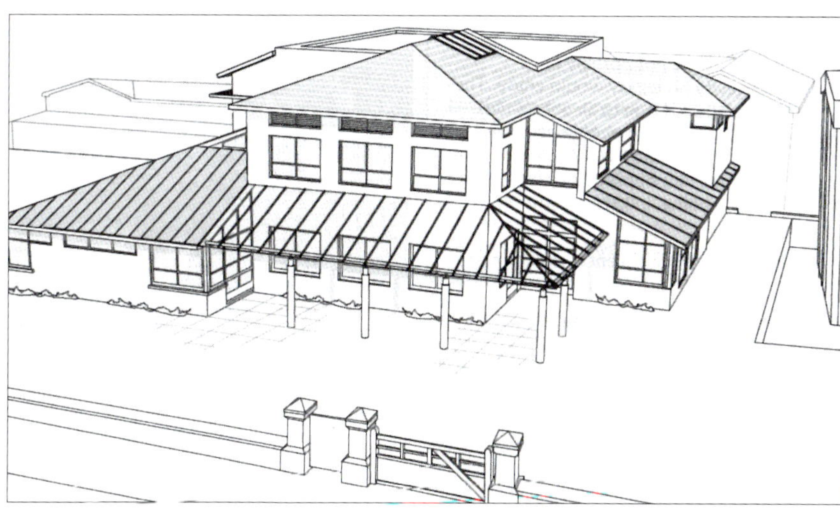

Artist's impression of the Junior Dept redevelopment, due to commence 2009/10.

Maynard Memories

Tregear Border 1946–1950

Joy Brealey (Trethewey)

I was a boarder at Tregear for four and a half years and vividly remember my first year there as it was so completely different from the life I had known.

Until the age of 12 I lived in Brazil, in a small gold-mining community where my father worked. I led a fairly solitary life which I enjoyed. I did not go to school as my father taught my brother and me in his spare time, setting us work to do each day which he would go over with us in the evening. My father was a mining engineer with no teaching experience and so the curriculum was rather strange and included Latin, Euclid, Architectural Drawing and even Shorthand. Then my family came to England and within a fortnight I was installed as a boarder at Tregear.

It was the summer term and I soon settled in to Upper 3P where the girls were so friendly and I made many long-lasting friendships. Everything was so new and strange to me but my classmates were keen to show me the ropes, which was a great help.

I did not fit in so well with life at Tregear. I was the only boarder in Upper 3P and was in a dormitory on the top floor with younger girls. They seemed so childish to me, playing at *being* horses instead of pretending to ride them. I was in the Junior Common Room which was a small room with lino on the floor, lockers, a table and a few wooden chairs. It looked out onto the tennis courts and Traceyville. The dining room was on one side and the kitchens on the other.

I remember on one occasion when the cupboard was opened a nest of new-born mice was found in a girl's beautifully-iced birthday cake!

There was no heating in the top dormitories and my first winter was the very severe one of 1946/47 which was quite a shock after living in the tropics. I remember becoming quite ill after playing in the snow for too long. We had to get ready for bed at 7pm and 'lights out' was at 7.30pm which seemed far too early to me.

In later years I moved down to two dormitories on the first floor. I particularly liked the small one which had only four beds instead of six or seven. On occasion we were invited to Miss Hindman's sitting room to listen to *Saturday Night Theatre* on the wireless which was a great treat.

In the dining room was a tuck cupboard which was not used very much (there was food rationing for a long time after the war) and I remember on one occasion when the cupboard was opened a nest of new-born mice was found in a girl's beautifully-iced birthday cake! I also recall the one time my dormitory had a midnight feast. We came downstairs and had it in the hall and it went off without a hitch.

Life was better when I was in the more comfortable senior sitting room. It had some carpet, a larger table, some easy chairs and a bigger window. The summer evenings were often spent playing tennis which was a bonus.

Occasionally girls were taken out for the day by visiting relatives or friends. It was a great treat to visit my cousin in Exeter or to go to my school friends' birthday parties. Once a week we would go to the small shops nearby to spend our sweet ration. I had £1 a term pocket money but would often have much of it left over at end of term.

Tregear Boarder 1956–1962

Sally Rutherford-Bunn (Baldwin)

In 1956 when I started at the Maynard, my first year in Lower 3 was as a day girl staying with my parents' friends who had a hotel at Broadclyst.

I became a boarder at Tregear in Upper 3. There were five dormitories: 6th, 5th, 3rd, 2nd and 1st (not sure why we never had a 4th dorm). A sitting room called The Playroom was shared between 5th and 6th dorms and we used to play Jacks, Pick-a-stick, Racing Demon or just read. The Common Room was for the rest of us, but the Sixth Form also had a study upstairs next door to the 6th dormitory.

Our first house mistress was called Miss Hindman (affectionately known as HB), and our matron was called Matron Merrills. I remember that HB had to have a stone hot water bottle put in her bed every night during winter and Matron Merrills had a boyfriend called Cyril who we used to try and catch a glimpse of when she had a day off!!

We had 'prayers' every night which consisted of a hymn, a prayer and notices. On Sunday evenings each dormitory took it in turns to take prayers.

Dormitory 6 in their Sunday uniform, in front of Tregear, just before setting off for St Leonard's Church, summer term 1950

Every Sunday we had to go to church and on special occasions like Remembrance Sunday we went to Exeter Cathedral. We all learnt deaf and dumb language so that we could 'talk' to each other during the sermons, which were always so boring! On Saturdays and Sundays we were allowed exeats (three per term), where our parents or friends could pick us up and take us out for the day. On Wednesdays and Sundays we had 'tuck tea' where we could use our own spreads and jams on our bread, instead of the usual lemon curd or strawberry jam. On Thursdays we were allowed to go down to the Mount Radford shops and buy sweets or pop [a fizzy drink such as lemonade], or anything that we needed, with our pocket money.

On the second to last night of each term we would put our pillow at the end of the bed and sleep that way around and on the penultimate night we re-arranged our beds into some kind of shape. Sometimes it was a rectangle where we put the beds head to toe all around the room, or in a T-shape with three beds across the room and four beds coming down from the middle, and sometimes it was a star when we put our seven bed heads into the middle so all our heads were together and we could talk easily!!

We finally got television in 1960 especially for the marriage of Princess Margaret to Anthony Armstrong-Jones [the first Royal wedding to be televised]. This was kept in the Headmistress's sitting room. We were allowed to watch television under supervision and of course Wimbledon was the most popular time when we all crowded in to watch it for two weeks.

One term when I was in 3rd dorm we decided not to take the Cod Liver Oil capsules which were given to us by Matron each morning but to save them up until the end of the term and see how many we could collect. I seem to remember it was over 500 and on the last day of term we threw them all out of the window on to the grass below! I also remember at about this time one Sunday morning when we all decided to smother ourselves in perfume; we each had a different one and when we went down to breakfast we certainly caused a stir!

When there was all the commotion about *Lady Chatterley's Lover*, Jane Cowper and I went down to Mount Radford, bought the book and secretly read it with a torch under our bed covers each night until we

Entire group of Tregear boarders with Miss Hindman, summer 1956

had finished it! When we were only 14 or 15 a group of us went to the cinema to see *Lolita* and, as you had to be at least 16 to get in, we practised for a week on new birth dates in case they asked us! One Saturday a couple of us snuck out and went to see Exeter City play a football match and, during the winter months, on Saturday afternoons, 1st and 2nd dorm used to have dancing classes with the Exeter School boarders – we were actually allowed to mix with boys!

At the end of most terms we had the obligatory Midnight Feast in our dormitory. We were very lucky as Suzanne Williams' parents owned a café and they used to supply us with cooked chicken, crisps, biscuits, chocolate and pop. When we were having these feasts, we used to unscrew the handle on the bedroom door so that no-one could come in and catch us!

I do feel that I had a very rounded education which has stood me in good stead for all of my life, and I look back at the times I spent at Tregear and the Maynard with fond memories. When I read what the Maynard offers today I am amazed!

Miss Mahy conducting the Choir at Speech Day 1961, in St George's Hall.

Tregear Boarder 1958

Margaret Guyver (Gilmore)

In January 1958 I became a temporary boarder in Tregear for two months while my mother went into hospital for a major operation. At 10 years old, I was in Form 2 and had been already at Traceyville for four terms, either travelling in from Exmouth daily by train or I had a lift with another girl whose father worked in Exeter. In those days it was thought that my father could not cope with the morning routine of getting me up, making me breakfast and getting me out of the house in time for whatever travel arrangement was at hand.

There were very few boarders from Traceyville. Most of the boarders were older and in the Main School. The vast majority of us were day girls and we felt rather sorry for the boarders who we felt were somewhat segregated from the rest of us and lived rather a cloistered life behind closed doors in Tregear. I'm afraid we looked on them as rather 'different'.

In Tregear, all meals were eaten in the Dining Room, half of what is now the ground floor Art Room, on the tennis court side of the building. Juniors (up to U3), sat at a large oblong table with Matron in charge; senior girls ate at their own tables. There was no evening meal for us, just tea at 5.30-ish which consisted of doorstep slices of white bread and butter, with tea or milk to drink. Jam, and possibly a cake, was allowed on Sundays. I expect the older girls had a cooked meal, but not the juniors. I don't remember about breakfast, it was probably toast, cereal and more tea, nor do I remember there being any fruit. There was, however, a strong smell of cabbage on the ground floor.

There was no evening meal for us, just tea at 5.30-ish which consisted of doorstep slices of white bread and butter, with tea or milk to drink. Jam, and possibly a cake, was allowed on Sundays.

The front entrance to Tregear was for parents and visitors, for the Sunday crocodile to church and for returning to the building when dropped off by car. At all other times, we came and left by a side door. When we went 'to school', we dressed in hats, coats and outdoor shoes, even for the short walk across the Tregear tennis courts.

Juniors had a small common room to the side of the building overlooking the tennis courts. It was intended that we should do prep in here, as there were few, if any, easy chairs and certainly no television. The older girls had their own common room next to the Dining Room into which we could go only by invitation. By the early 1960s, there was a TV set in there. As day girls, we used to sneak in and watch the Wimbledon Tennis Championship matches.

I slept in a dormitory on the second floor, in what is now a Music Room. There was a good view of the Cathedral but the Bobby's/Debenhams building [now empty] had not yet been built. I think there were six of us juniors. Lights-out was 9pm; I think the morning bell went at 7am. Beds had to be immaculately made and dormitories tidied straight after breakfast. Inspections were carried out; these included the tidiness of our drawers and cupboards. One cuddly toy was placed lying to attention on each bed. Before and after school we had morning and evening prayers which were taken on the first floor landing by Miss Hindman, who was in charge of Tregear. All girls were expected to attend.

Supervised by Matron, all washing, including our socks and handkerchiefs, was bundled up and sent to an external laundry on Thursdays and returned a week later (in brown paper parcels tied up with string). All the brown paper had to be carefully folded up and the string coiled and given back to Matron for next time.

The main change to my routine as a day girl was that I was expected to return to Tregear at all times when not in class, except at morning break. I had made my own friends amongst the day girls so I found this very frustrating. On my first day as a boarder, I queued with my friends as usual to go into the Traceyville end of the canteen for lunch, but someone sent for me and I had to don hat and coat and return to Tregear for the entire lunch hour.

Every other Thursday, after the fortnightly class lists were read out in assembly, the boarders were quizzed at tea about their results, so those getting a low mark (D or Fail) were shamed once more.

Once a week (again on Thursdays), after school, we were allowed to go to the shops in Magdalen Road, to stock up on chocolate and comics. I can remember the sense of freedom I felt on that short expedition, and the relief of being back in the 'real' world. I cannot remember what was expected of us on Saturdays. Perhaps I did go home then. On Sundays, all the regular boarders put on their Sunday suits (navy) and hats (a slightly different model to the everyday winter soup-plate ones). About 30 to 40 of us walked in a crocodile to St Leonard's Church for the morning service, where we filled several pews. After lunch, those who were not being taken out by their families went back to church for Crusaders, a church-based organisation run by St Leonard's for young people. Somehow I managed not to be part of this.

Sixth Form boarders relaxing outside Tregear, c1957. The large building behind is the Dining Centre which was pulled down in 1990 to make way for the Pring building.

My short time at Tregear was not the happiest episode in my life but the discipline was probably 'good for me'. It also cured me of ever wanting to go to full-time boarding school. I suppose I imagined that Tregear would be more like a school story, that there would be midnight feasts and a chance to rescue my dorm mates from some bizarre fate. We did giggle a bit after lights out, but there were certainly no midnight feasts while I was there and only one fire practice. I never did understand the policy of separating the boarders from their daytime classmates at lunchtime, except that at about that time, there was pressure on space in the main canteen and day girls who lived close to school were asked if they could go home for lunch. The younger Tregear boarders certainly lived a cloistered existence by today's standards but perhaps I saw things a bit differently as I was only boarding for a short while.

Form 2 arriving at the West Door of Exeter Cathedral for Tercentenary Thanksgiving Service, 1958

Two Celebratory Years

G W Sutcliffe, taken from the 1977 school magazine

(Miss Sutcliffe was Head of Junior School 1935–1954)

Jubilee Year 1936

At that time Traceyville was an ordinary dwelling house, with a small patch of tarmac in front, two or three shrubberies, very useful for hide-and-seek and play acting, flower borders besides the walls, and a large patch of grass at the back, 'Traceyville Grass'. The largest room was the Kindergarten Room, which we used as a Hall, and where we assembled for Prayers, except on the one day each week when we went to the Main School for Prayers and Mark Lists. There were no facilities for school dinners and as far as I can remember, I think we used to have dinner in a room above the old kitchen, in the Main School. This room had a hoist. You can imagine what it meant on wet days. We used one of the Main School cloakrooms, where it was very difficult to keep track of the children's coats and shoes. The Kindergarten Room was very popular for plays and concerts, as it had sliding doors, which took the place of curtains.

There were both boys and girls in Traceyville. I taught the Kindergarten and Transition, usually 30 children, aged about four and a half to seven years. At Christmas we used to have a big party in the Main School Hall, with a huge Christmas tree, with real candles and toys for 'Poor Children' at its base. There was a present for each child in Traceyville, too, and it is hard to believe now that these could then be bought for a penny each. Parents were invited to hear the children sing carols, when the candles were lighted. Fire precautions were very strict. Helpers with wet sponges on the ends of long canes watched, and put out immediately any candle that showed signs of guttering.

Kindergarten class in Traceyville, c1940

In the summer I used to organize a 'Farm Picnic' for the Kindergarten and Transition. This involved a visit to a farm, where we saw cows milked, by hand in those days, and pigs fed, when the noise was a shock to the children. We always tried to look at the hay, and a field of corn, because after our Harvest Festival in the autumn term, we always tried to crush wheat between stones and we made bread with brown flour. We had to take it to the Main School kitchen to be cooked.

In 1936, I had been in charge of Traceyville just over a year only, but the then Headmistress, Miss Ryan, and myself had already begun planning for a new building. It amazes me now to remember how happy we all were in the old one and what good work was done in spite of the cramped conditions thanks to my wonderful staff.

1952–1953

Things were very different at the time of the Queen's Accession and Coronation. The extended Traceyville building completely transformed the Junior School. No boys were admitted after 1949; I missed them very much. The Kindergarten and Transition had lessons in the afternoon. That meant the provision of more dinners. What is now [in 1977] the Transition cloakroom was made into a kitchen in which Cook (Mrs Richards), and her assistant (Mrs Holmes) used to prepare appetizing meals. I can still remember her pancakes on Pancake Day. These meals were served to Form 2 in the Hall and to the rest of the Junior School in the Kindergarten. The tables were laid by the children and cleared by them, too. How much nicer it was than trailing over to the Main School in all weathers! The children were able to play on Traceyville grass and there was still room in the grounds for Form 2 to have small gardens of their own. The Hall in Traceyville with its sliding doors and unsplinterable floor was a delight and bare-footed physical training and dancing were popular.

Our timetable was still dovetailed with that of the Main School and during the O- and A-level examinations, we had difficulty in imposing a suitable standard of noiseless behaviour on our young children. The Junior School Sports, our Harvest Festival, and the Christmas Party were still important highlights of our School Year, and every child continued to have a small present from the Christmas Tree although the cost had risen to 2d. or even to 4d [1.5p].

But how exactly we celebrated the Coronation, I cannot remember, for that week the School was empty.

The War Years

Kathleen Boreham (Born), 1936–1942, Head Girl 1941–1942

I started at the Maynard in 1936 as a boarder at Tregear having previously been at a small preparatory school in Kingsbridge. There was no provision for secondary education for girls in the South Hams in those days, so boarding was the only option. It was a big change! Full school days, supervised prep in the boarding house each night under the eagle eye of Miss Berney but quite a lot of treats. Picnics at Budleigh Salterton and Bickleigh Bridge, shopping in Exeter on Saturday mornings, a crocodile to the Cathedral on Sundays, informal hockey on Tregear lawn at weekends, but only after we had done our supervised mending with matron. She had been known to cut out a darn from a black stocking if it wasn't good enough by her standard. I remember one day she accused me of wearing lipstick. She took me into the bathroom and scrubbed my lips. All to no avail of course as I didn't even own a lipstick. Every night in winter two of us had to fill about 20 hot water bottles from huge heavy black kettles. I don't remember anyone getting scalded. Health and Safety would have a fit today.

1st XI Hockey Team, c1938/39 (Kathleen Born, back row, 2nd from right)

1st XI Cricket Team, 1941 (Kathleen Born, back row 4th from left)

I think I caused a minor sensation when I was in Upper 4 by contracting typhoid and being *very* ill. Friends told me I was prayed for in school prayers. I ended up in Exeter isolation hospital for four months with a boy from another school and a Spanish fisherman who was interned in Exeter prison. He had been picked up by the Royal Navy during the Spanish civil war. Typhoid caused the health authorities quite a headache but no link was ever found.

The outbreak of war meant more restrictions; parent visiting was very much reduced due to petrol rationing and we became very reliant on letters. There were gas mask practices in class and sitting for a whole lesson in a gas mask was very stifling. In the evening we had to knit khaki socks and I learned to turn a heel. An air raid shelter was built under the 'New Grass', lined with wood and lit by hanging storm lanterns. This was put to the test on the night of Sunday, 3rd May 1942 when the sirens went at about 1.45am and we all trooped down to the trench. There we stayed with the noise of bomber engines, the deafening anti-aircraft guns and the patter of shrapnel and incendiary bombs in lines, like someone running across the grass above. The blast from five high explosive bombs, all of which fell in our grounds, set the lanterns swinging and the bomb nearest us blew out all the lanterns leaving us in darkness. I took a strictly forbidden look from the entrance to our shelter for only a few seconds (I am quoting from my diary). The sky was bright orange and the town was behind a line of fire. Where Tregear stood was just a mass of smoke and sparks and there was the noise of breaking glass. Everything seemed to be moving and it was very windy. The Vicarage, yards away, was on fire and there was creaking as bits crashed down (the family were with us in our trench).

Upper 5, 1939, outside what is now the main entrance

In the morning we walked, still in our night clothes, in a crocodile to Exeter School, stepping over hoses and skirting piles of rubble all the way. There we were given a very welcome breakfast and put to bed in their dormitories for a couple of hours. A little later some of us returned to Tregear and were told to collect what we could from the dormitory before going home. Looking back I can hardly believe this was allowed. There were no windows left and the hall was full of rubble. There was water coming through the ceiling. We picked our way up to dormitory 5 on the top floor but the door wouldn't open. We pushed and shoved until the smallest of us, Anne Booker, could squeeze in, and she managed to shift the rubble from the inside. Our clothes were all buried but I dragged some out from among the bricks and plaster and wrapped them in a towel. As we went downstairs we saw the crater in the double tennis court and all the earth thrown up with an unaccountable kitchen chair perched on top. We realized then that we were lucky to be alive.

As we went downstairs we saw the crater in the double tennis court and all the earth thrown up with an unaccountable kitchen chair perched on top. We realized then that we were lucky to be alive.

I can't remember getting back to Kingsbridge but I do remember bursting into tears at the sight of my father hurrying along the platform to meet me.

When things settled down the School was divided up amongst other schools and I, with some other Sixth Formers, was sent to Hele's School for boys. Co-education was an unheard of thing then. Recently I met a Hele's old boy who remembered the lecture they had from the headmaster on how to behave when the six Maynard girls came!

The Post War society was formed during the war for the Sixth Form. Hele's, Dover College (evacuated), Bishop Blackall, Blundell's, Exeter School and maybe others, all sent representatives to discuss future post-war issues. This was very forward-looking in the dark days of 1942. I can't remember what was discussed but we took it all very seriously – as well as enjoying residential weekends at Blundell's.

Finally, I must pay tribute to the Headmistress Miss Ryan, affectionately known as Elsie May, who did me the honour of inviting me to be Head Girl. She was a constant encouragement to me and I became very fond of her. She came to the Maynard from Cheltenham Ladies' College. Little did I know then that my own four daughters would one day go there as day girls.

The War Years

Rosemary Carrington (Harrison-Ainsworth)
Tregear boarder from Spring Term 1941 (aged 15) to Summer Term 1942

Bomb damage to the north end (Room 14) of main school building. In the foreground is the statue of a young dancing girl erected in memory of pupil Rose Michelmore who had died, aged 5, in 1931. The cornucopia that she carried over her head was blown away in the bomb blast. Today 'Rosie' , as she is affectionately known, resides in the Garden of Reflection, an area of quiet contemplation for the whole school community; built in memory of pupil Emily Webster, who died in the 2004 Ufton Nervet train crash.

The most vivid memory of my time at the Maynard is undoubtedly the night of the blitz. I arrived back at school a few days late for the beginning of the summer term (having had mumps and complications), and the blitz was that very night. Due, I think, to some smaller air raids earlier on and the threat of ones to come we were all sleeping on the ground floor, on beds packed closely together like sardines in two rows in the junior common room. Every night we had by our beds Burberrys, boots, gas masks and a sweater.

We were woken by the air raid alarm and all went into the underground shelter in the school grounds, very close to Tregear. The shelter must have been quite large and as far as I remember we sat on benches around the edge by the light of hurricane lamps or torches. I do not remember how long we had been there when suddenly everyone from the other boarding house, Summerlands, appeared. The raid was still in progress but their house had been hit and was on fire; their shelter was not underground and they were in imminent danger. They had had to run from their house in Heavitree Road down Spicer Road to Tregear and I can still picture their wide-eyed and startled faces.

When morning came and the raid had ended we all walked up to Exeter School. It was a beautiful sunny day and there was smoke still coming from damaged houses as we walked by, still in our night-clothes. When we arrived we were taken to the boys' dormitories – they had been turned out of their beds – and I remember being delighted climbing into a still warm bed! Later in the day relieved parents were able to drive into Exeter to take us home. My home was 17 miles away, near Whiddon Down, and they had heard the thuds from falling bombs and seen the red glow in the sky and knew it was Exeter.

Because of the bomb damage all the boarders were dispersed (I stayed with a doctor's family), and my form and probably others used Exeter School. I do not recall ever returning to the Maynard School itself as I left at the end of that term after taking my Higher Certificate.

The War Years

Helen Harris (Warren) 1939–1944

I was a day girl during the years of the Second World War, and a boarder, at Summerlands in Heavitree Road, from September 1939 to the time of the Blitz.

Exeter had suffered a more minor air raid in the latter part of April, during our school Easter holidays. Because of this we were required to delay our return to school for some days as the boarding house was without supplies of water and gas. It was therefore the evening of Sunday, 3rd May when my parents took me back to school for the summer term, together with all my necessary belongings – school uniform, a few new items (including a particularly pretty 'mufti' dress made from material obtained with precious clothes rationing coupons), and all my school books filled with the notes I was accumulating for School Certificate exams in the following year. I was then 15 years old.

Summerlands Boarders, with staff and matron, c1935/36

Since the start of the war we had had to have regular surprise air raid practices. From 1940 there was a large underground shelter in the school grounds to which we had to go. The routine was that every night we would place trousers, jumper, raincoat, outdoor shoes, and gas mask, on the bedside chair. Then, every week or so, after we were in bed, the shrill and startling whistle would suddenly be sounded and out we would jump, don our clothes, run downstairs, out across Heavitree Road and along Spicer Road to the school shelter. We would of course be counted, and the exercise timed. No one appeared to consider what passers-by might be thinking on those light summer evenings at seeing 30 or so young females tearing along in motley-covered night attire. A year later, however, a shelter was built for our own use, very close to the house in the garden at the back. This avoided the nocturnal sprint, and I do not recall practices then being so frequent.

Therefore, we were all reasonably prepared as to what we should do when we were awakened by air raid sirens – and doubtless also the whistle – a short while after midnight on 4th May. We all trooped down to the shelter in the garden, to the sound of approaching aircraft.

This shelter was only half below ground, built of concrete blocks. It was long and fairly narrow, with seats along the sides, duckboards for feet, and at the far end – in case of need – an Elsan closet, discreetly screened. I can still remember the smell of damp concrete and hurricane oil lamp that pervaded. I was seated near the door, on the right hand side, and there would have been probably just over 30 of us, including housemistress and matron, filling the shelter.

Soon proceedings became decidedly noisy with increasing bangs, some of them very near. I suppose we had a feeling of fear but I do not particularly remember. I do recall one of the younger girls asking the mistress if she should pray, and as she said aloud the Lord's Prayer those of us near her I am sure joined her in our hearts.

Presently the housemistress slightly opened the door and told us that the house was alight and that there were green flares 'all over the garden'. I could see this myself from where I was sitting, and this seemed to increase potential danger. I particularly recall briefly looking up at the part of the building – on the top floor – where I had been sleeping, and seeing the flames pouring up to the sky and the roof collapsing, and thinking that that was the end of my new dress and all my school papers and other things.

Eventually the situation became quieter and soon an air raid warden came to the shelter door. He said

I particularly recall briefly looking up at the part of the building where I had been sleeping, and seeing the flames pouring up to the sky and the roof collapsing, and thinking that that was the end of my new dress and all my school papers and other things.

that we must move immediately because of danger from the burning house, and he led us to a terraced house in Lower Summerlands. This would probably have been between 3 and 4am. The people in the house accepted our 'invasion' with great calm and were most kind, giving us cups of tea and fruit cake, but it was not long before we had to move from there also, because a house just two or three doors away was on fire. So off we trooped for the quarter-mile to the School shelter, where we found the Tregear girls still installed. By this time the raid was long over and dawn arriving. Doubtless there had been some communication between the authorities, and the decision was taken for us to go up to Exeter School as a staging-post. It was now daylight and so we made our way – two and two in the customary orderly 'crocodile' mode of progression – out of the school environs and up Magdalen Road. By the time of our arrival – perhaps around 6am – the boys had been instructed to vacate their dormitories, and we girls sank into their still-warm beds, two girls to each, for a 'rest'!

I don't think any of us actually slept, but I suppose it kept us out of the way until the boys could be fed, and a second breakfast kindly prepared for all of us. When this was ready and we were all downstairs and tucking in, a message came for me that my father had arrived to take me home. He and my mother, at Tiverton, had with great anxiety watched the blaze in the sky during the night. My father wasted no time in driving to Exeter, fortunately getting through before large-scale closure of roads, driving over glass, debris, and hoses in the process. As he approached the boarding house he faced with horror the gaunt, blackened, skeletal, denuded wall structures and charred, smouldering remains within. Then, as he got nearer, he saw a notice attached to the gate by the thoughtful housemistress: 'ALL GIRLS SAFELY EVACUATED TO EXETER SCHOOL'. It was a strange drive back to Tiverton – this time without any luggage – and an emotional reunion with my mother.

Roberta Thomas and two friends in the garden at Summerlands, 1939

School did not resume for a further week or so. Although the main school building, and Tregear, had survived, the School suffered a certain amount of damage. Parts of the School were repaired fairly quickly – as the headmistress, Miss Ryan later said 'thanks to day after day of fine weather' – sufficiently for use in that summer term, while a number of us and our staff were accommodated at Bishop Blackall School, on a shift system – they did their work in prolonged mornings; we started at 1.30 pm and continued until 5.30. As we moved about Exeter in those days the extent to which the poor city and its people had suffered became all too apparent.

Celebrating 350 years

Quotations from the Big Reunion Weekend Visitors' Book

Living Logo

Miss Murdin helping to lay the foundations of the Murdin Link, and later opening the new building.

'A privileged opportunity to be here and see everyone.'
(left 1973)

'Great to catch up with the year – lunch much improved on those days!'
(left 1968)

'A Celebration of Art' Exhibition

Governors' 350th Dinner at Tuckers' Hall, with Headmistress Dr Daphne West, centre

Two Lower 5 Haberdashers in house colours!

Traditional races are always fun

Haberdashers in foreground, Merchants behind, enjoying their picnic lunch in glorious weather

'The longer I'm away, the more I appreciate the values that Maynard instilled and the great education we all received.'
(left 1991)

'It was worth coming all the way from Australia to catch up with old friends.'
(left 1962)

Down to the last few in Musical Statues

A packed Cathedral for the Gala Concert

Thanksgiving Service —
a time to reflect

'Well worth travelling 3,000 miles! Wonderful memories.'
(left 1968)

'Wonderful! So glad I came.'
(left 1956)

Rousing finale at the Gala Concert

'A day to always remember.'
(left 1956)

'Entirely appropriate that the chemistry lab is now the kitchen!'
(left 1956)

Sixth Form cake stall at the Fête

Seniors demonstrating their Science Timeline ideas to the Juniors

Miss Millar, Head of PE, amazed by Science

Sixth Formers, Sarah Tresidder and Katy Pearce, sporting the 'mad professor' look for their Science Timeline presentation

'Amazed at how much is still recognisable.'
(left 1947)

'Fascinating, wouldn't have missed it for the world.'
(left 1959)

A wonderful evening at the 350th Anniversary Ball

(Photographs courtesy Matt Lewis)

'So much changed yet so much the same.'
(left 1968)

'Lovely to be surrounded by friends from the past.'
(left 1973)

'Thank you for a wonderful day of memories.'
(left 1956)

The 350th Big Reunion
An unforgettable weekend of memories and renewing old friendships

Reunion photographs courtesy Robin Jones and © Quay Studios

'After 70 years – how lovely to see the school.'
(left 1939)

'Fifty years "flew away".'
(left 1957)

'Lots of memories – once a Maynardian, always a Maynardian!'
(left 1986)

The War Years

Janet Robb (1939–1946, 1948–49)

A little-known event in the history of the Maynard School happened in our garden at Quarrylands at the top of Dunsford Hill. Following the Exeter Blitz in May 1942 when the School was badly damaged, my mother arranged for Miss Sutcliffe, head of Traceyville, to hold a small school in our garden during the mornings of that summer term. I was 10 and went to Bishop Blackall School in the afternoons so was able to help Miss Sutcliffe, who came on her bicycle, in the mornings. The school was attended by my brother Geoffrey who was aged six at the time, together with three or four other children who lived locally, including Jane Gairdner [sic] who came from Ide and Brenda McGurran from the bottom of Dunsford Hill. Miss Sutcliffe brought up the cardboard 'money' from school and Geoffrey was in charge of 'The Bank'. I ran a shop with garden produce and appropriate notices: 'Queue here', 'Please bring back the bags'! I know we made things from clay and altogether had an enjoyable summer while the School was closed.

Maynard children at the 'Quarrylands school' during the war

Janet Robb running her wartime 'shop'

Old Maynardian boy, Geoffrey Robb, in charge of 'The Bank'

An Old Boy

Geoffrey Robb, brother of Janet (1942–1944)

In 1942, when the local kindergarten was bombed, a few younger brothers of sisters who were already there were admitted to the Maynard School. I was one of those fortunate few who, at the age of five, entered the kindergarten under the care of Miss Sutcliffe. That year seemed to be mostly play but I remember having to pass a shoelace-tying test. I think I taught myself as I tied my laces then (and still do), in a completely different way to everyone else. Miss Sutcliffe, in her pragmatic way, said 'Well, it seems to work, so I'll pass you'.

Transition was more demanding as we were then into joined-up Writing, Arithmetic and simple Geometry. When the air-raid sirens went, we all had to get under our desks. We all went over to the main school for lunch, past some pretty intimidating girls playing tennis, who clearly didn't think much of the small fry from the kindergarten. There was an obligatory rest after lunch on mats which we had to unroll.

What I remember clearly is, at the age of six, getting myself home from school. I went down the main drive, up Barnfield Road and watched the telegraph boys in smart uniforms get on their bikes or (better still), motorbikes and dash off with their precious cargo from the telegraph office where Barnfield Road joins Southernhay. That, I thought, was the job for me when I grew up – perhaps just as well I changed my mind! I know I walked through Cathedral Close and up St Martin's Lane to the High Street, where there was a branch of Hill, Palmer and Edwards opposite the end of Queen Street. I would usually buy a penny bun, a delicious stodgy but sweet confection with, if you were lucky, a few currants and sultanas. I was so outraged when they increased the price to a penny farthing that I stopped buying them for a week, thinking that might be the way to combat this inflationary spiral, but of course my boycott had no effect; I got hungry and a penny farthing it had to be.

Traceyville display, 1941

I could catch either the Redhills or the Broadway bus, which both went to the bottom of Dunsford Hill, which I walked up to get home.

To my embarrassment now (but not then), one of my reports said, among other things: 'He must learn not to interfere with the girls'. By then, I think the boys had outstayed their welcome and at the age of seven I went with the others to Exeter School.

Beacon School in Teignmouth and Epsom College followed on from Exeter School and I read Medicine at Bristol. After working in Cape Town (among other places), I returned to Epsom as a physician in 1974. I have been enormously happy there and among many others I had the privilege of treating a niece of Miss Ryan some years ago.

Staff play, *Arms and the Man*, c1944

The Rennes Exchange 1965–2005

How It Began

Mrs Frances Stephens (Miss Martin)

One of the most enjoyable aspects of teaching French is taking your pupils to France, and so, in the autumn of 1965, I asked Miss Bradley if we could organise a school exchange. One of the University staff suggested that we should approach L'Immaculée-Conception, a well-established Roman Catholic convent school in Rennes, Exeter's twin city. I wrote to la Mère-Supérieure, outlining the possibilities for an exchange and suggesting that I might go over to discuss the project.

It was a weekend I shall never forget! I was made so welcome by the most delightful Community of Sisters. We agreed that the Maynard group should spend three weeks in Rennes at Easter and receive the French party back at the end of the summer term, thus allowing both groups to experience a few days of school life with their 'correspondantes'. Soeur Louise-Marie Cornu was to be responsible for the French party and became a tower of strength. I cannot speak too highly of her enthusiasm, her co-operation and her efficiency. Together we composed an application form, asking for photos and as much information as possible about the girls and their families. I remember laying all the forms out on the floor and trying to choose the best partnerships. Not easy!

During the next few months letters were exchanged. Useful phrases were learnt for various situations. (*'C'est délicieux mais je n'ai plus faim.' 'Je ne me sens pas très bien. J'ai la diarrhée.'*) At last we set off. I was determined that our party should arrive dressed respectably and forbade the girls to wear trousers for the crossing. How could I have been so unreasonable and old fashioned?! Our coach arrived late at night and we were greeted by a crowd of parents all eager to claim their visitor. I still admire the fortitude of those pioneers as they disappeared into the unknown. The exchange was under way!

In 1985 we celebrated the 20th anniversary of the exchange and it was noted then that over a thousand young people had taken part. At a ceremony in Rennes, Soeur Louise-Marie and I were presented with 'la Médaille de la Ville de Rennes' as Founders of the Exchange. I felt so proud for everybody who had been involved!

Soeur Louise-Marie and I met 43 years ago and we remain the best of friends. When I spoke to her about this book, she sent records of the main events over the past years and it has been lovely to recall memories of what she describes as 'ces années merveilleuses'. For me too, they were wonderful years.'

Channel crossing en route to Rennes 1969

1970 Onwards

Mrs Madeleine (Pip) Davis

When I joined the Maynard School Staff in 1970, the Rennes Exchange was already well established, with numbers increasing yearly. It was at this time that Exeter School, under the leadership of Mr Bob Brooks, joined the exchange, since the convent had become mixed! Helping with and then taking over the organisation and running of the French exchange was a marvellous and challenging experience and remembering it brings back many good memories, in spite of the odd crisis at the time! Here are just a few of both:

- Staying at the convent with the Sisters and feeling honoured as an English 'lay' teacher, to be accepted into their community.
- The long, long, journey by coach and boat to Rennes (13 hours), and the silence that descended on the coach in the last hour as our charges approached the unknown …

- Meeting up with the pupils on the trips and on the journey home, when they would recount the 'highs' and 'lows' of their stay with great excitement. It was a privilege to be party to this and to really get to know the group as individuals and observe their confidence and independence grow. It made it all worthwhile.
- On the outing to Mont St Michel one year with Mr Harry Guest, languages teacher from Exeter School, seeing some people way out on the mud flats and panicking in case they were ours – the tide comes in faster than a galloping horse, and the telescope was useless!
- Coping with the realities of an outbreak of *la fièvre aphteuse* (foot and mouth disease), in the Rennes area, when there were pupils going *from* an English farm *to* a French one and back again.
- Having a real French priest (Le Père Restif) to stay with us at our home and enjoying a day out at Saunton Sands with him. And then entertaining the Soeurs every summer. There was always much laughter and they were so appreciative.

When I look back, I shudder at the apparent risks we took and the level of responsibility involved , but it was worth it. And for me too, Soeur Louise-Marie is a friend for life.'

Former Pupils' Memories of the French Exchange

In the school magazine report of the Rennes Exchange in 1976, Siân Hanson, to whom her partner family, the Famille Thomas, has become like a second family, then aged 14 and in Upper 4, wrote:

'The first week was the most difficult as far as language problems were concerned. Later in my stay, when I knew the family better, it gave me a great sense of achievement when I found I could understand most of what was said – at the beginning I could only distinguish single words or at most, small phrases.'

As for attending lessons in French of one hour length, not only were they really difficult to follow, but: "Have you ever tried learning algebraic fractions in French?"'

Nicola von Schreiber (Gibbs)

'I remember as though it were yesterday my first sight of my French exchange family peering into the windows of our coach as it arrived in Rennes, and the relief of recognising each other from the photos. Theirs was the first flat I'd ever been inside. There were many firsts on that trip: tasting artichokes, plain yoghurt with sugar, pain au chocolat, Orangina. Coping with the language was so intense; I doubt I spoke more than a few words the first week, in spite of Madame urging me to practise more – I was putting so much effort into just understanding what I heard, which ever since makes me empathise with foreign visitors. It was a Eureka moment when my French girl's cousin told us *"On y va!"*; another when a smaller cousin took to calling me *"mon Anglaise"* and I knew I was getting an insight into French as it is actually used rather than what we learned in the classroom. I hadn't expected that, so far, those were my only chances to see the Bayeux Tapestry, Mont St Michel or the beaches of Brittany. And it wasn't until my own daughter went on her first exchange that I appreciated the creative thinking and generous giving of time that the adults had put into giving us this adventure.'

Lunch at L'Immaculée, c1968

Alison Organ (Jones)

'I suppose you could say that I was a successful product of the Rennes exchange, because I went three times in all, and went on to study French at university and become a French teacher. It was however, quite a scary experience! We stayed for three weeks, a length of time unheard of for exchanges nowadays. Here is a random selection of memories, good and bad, gleaned from the diaries I wrote at the time (I seemed to spend a lot of time writing up my *journal* in French for Mrs Davis!):

- I still remember arriving in Rennes late at night after a tiring journey and being subjected to what felt like a cattle market. As we got off the coach and huddled together in the cold and the dark, we were 'picked off' one by one as the French families identified their guests and carried them away.
- Having three helpings of the first course during our first *dîner*, thinking that was all we were getting, only to be given a plateful of meat followed by a plateful of veg, then salad, then cheese, then dessert.
- Having to watch the French family dip stale baguette spread with butter in their morning coffee or hot chocolate, and seeing the butter melt and spread in greasy globules over the surface.
- Interminable guided tours round the *Palais de Justice* and other worthy sites (I don't think as 14-year-olds we appreciated the finer points of French architecture!)
- Getting homesick by the middle of the third week, despite a never-ending flow of letters to and from family and friends.
- Being taken to Paris to stay in a luxury flat with my exchange partner's aunt, where they had a maid whom they summoned with a bell!
- My first experience of a *crêperie*, quite a revelation to someone who thought you could only eat pancakes with sugar and lemon.
- Watching England win the Eurovision song contest (even though it was the Brotherhood of Man!).
- The feeling of accomplishment as I gradually felt I could understand my host family and make myself understood.

As teenagers we had no inkling of the amount of work that went into organising trips like this; I am just grateful in retrospect that our teachers were willing to commit that amount of time and effort to a "holiday" which, while relatively traumatic at the outset, gave us a real sense of achievement and independence.'

The Rennes Exchange lasted for some 40 years, latterly with the English pupils going to Rennes in July and the French pupils visiting Exeter at Easter in alternate years, and, more recently still, a shortened length of stay. Many members of staff contributed to the exchange over those 40 years and amongst those to whom the exchange was indebted are included Miss Sheila Laycock, Miss Elisabeth Goulden (now Mrs Reardon), Miss Margaret Tucker, Mrs Marie-Edith Cameron, Mrs Maggie Coaton and Mrs Odile Saunders. And last, but not least, thanks to all the real heroes, the hundreds and hundreds of you brave former pupils for being prepared to step out of the comfort zone and take part! No e-mail or mobile phones back in the early days, and phoning England was a costly and lengthy process! You all certainly did your bit towards encouraging Anglo-French friendship.

Footnote

Interestingly, in the 1924–25 school magazine the following letter appears, from Old Girl, Agatha Booker:

Dear Madam

I have recently been much interested in arranging exchanges between English boys and girls and French or German boys and girls. I am personally in touch with several people in France, Germany and Austria, who would be glad to take an English girl for a month or six weeks in summer in exchange for a French or German girl. The exchange may be consecutive or simultaneous.

I also hear of posts for English women in various parts of Europe.

At present, I know of a very nice family in the country near Buda-Pest [sic] who want an Englishwoman as a companion and governess to two boys (aged about 4 and 6). A knowledge of German is useful, but not essential.

Further, I know of a girl in Innsbruck who wishes to come to England for three months or so next spring in exchange for an English girl. I also know of a boy in Brittany who wishes to come to England in exchange for a boy or girl from England.

If anyone cares to know more about these, would she write to me at the above address.

Whether anything came of this enquiry is not recorded.

Ten Tors

Pat Read, Member of PE Department 1976–1994

The Maynard first became involved with the Ten Tors event in the late 1970s, when the School entered just one team for the 35-mile expedition. This team consisted of girls from the Sixth Form, and within two years, because of a demand for places, the School entered two 35-mile teams, both involving Sixth Form girls. The rules at that time stated that girls of 16/17 could take part in the 35-mile event, as their first expedition, but in 1989 the Army decided that there should be an equality of the sexes, and anyone aged 16/17 had to undertake the 45-mile distance. This came as a considerable shock to the girls who had started that season's training 'thinking 35-miles', only to have to re-think '45-miles'! However, with true Maynardian grit and determination they were not deterred, and for the first time, the Maynard entered two 45-mile teams. That year also, the girls made scarlet sweatshirts for members of both teams, and for all the helpers as well. Each was printed with an individually chosen logo, drawn by a very talented Lower Sixth artist. (I still have mine and wear it often, and know of two others still worn regularly.)

Now, of course, was the time to enter a 35-mile team taken from Lower 5 (the members of which had been agitating to do this for some years), so, in 1990, off we went, and entered teams for both the 35-mile and 45-mile events. Each year our allocation depended upon the Army's rationing system, but generally we were able to enter three Maynard teams involving both distances. The school allowed us to buy more of the necessary training equipment, and we had some very generous donations from parents and friends, including a 'walkie-talkie' set, which was a wonderful asset (no mobile phones in those days), and which helped us to keep in touch with our back-up vehicles, and base camp.

There were 12 training sessions, which included four weekend camps, several day walks, the 24-mile Abbots Way Walk, from Buckfast to Tavistock (which takes place on the first Sunday in October), and the 27-mile OATS (Okehampton Adventure Training Scheme), from New Waste, near Cornwood to Okehampton (which takes place on the first Sunday in April). The Sixth Form also did a half day walk on a Tuesday afternoon from Combestone Tor to Trowlesworthy Tors. By now we had joined forces with St Margaret's and Exeter School for some of our training weekends, and the element of competition between the schools was an incentive! ('BUT always remember, the Ten Tors event is NOT a race!!') I have to add, that in those days, the Lower Sixth had no such horrors as AS-levels and had some breathing space between the public exams, which allowed them more time for training, or for generally being able to choose to do 'their own thing' for a bit.

Memories? Weather! Fog, rain, gales, heat and, memorably, snow on one April Fool's Day. The crossing of boggy ground, and being asked if I too was sinking. Asking teams for their whereabouts in a fog, to be met by worried looks, and whispers: 'If she doesn't know, how are we going to get back?' Explain that I do know, but that they must know too! The imaginative recipes thought up for Trangia [a particular type of camping stove] cooking, the fights with flapping tents, the many tumbles into rivers, the blisters, the lack of sleep, the anxiety when a team was 'mislaid', the get-togethers in a pub at the end of a day's training, everyone warm and safe, and, of course, the event itself. That wake-up call (*Chariots of Fire*, or *Daybreak*), the Start, after the very moving Ten Tors prayer (always resulting in a lump in my throat), the amazing sight of hundreds of young people setting off on that big adventure, and the moment when none of them was left! The all day (and night!) checking on progress on 'leader boards' (no computer screens then), times and positions written up by weary soldiers, and Team Managers all jostling and pushing in a very small tented area to see what was happening 'out there'. The excitement of seeing the returning teams coming over the hill; the thrill of their safe and successful return.

Over the years I have been amazed and impressed by the sheer guts of each girl. 'Never give up', I used to say, and they never did.

I must also mention the Special Event for handicapped youngsters who, with tremendous courage, take part over various distances, and several Maynard girls have helped support, or walk with the disabled. I thank them for that commitment, and I know that it was an experience they will not forget. One young boy will always remain in my memory, as he took all day to do seven miles, walking with a frame, dragging one foot after the other. His joy as he received his medal was unbelievable.

Over the years I have been amazed and impressed by the sheer guts of each girl. 'Never give up', I used to say, and they never did. Only once have teams been forced to stop*, due to heavy snow and Army orders. The 45-

mile team (and that year also a Maynard 55-mile team), were both at Sittaford Tor and going well, when orders were issued. It took five hours for the Army to bring them back to Okehampton, and they could have walked back in under that time! Frustrating! Some of those involved in the 55-mile team did it again the following year, completing successfully this time. They were not to be beaten! Maynard 35-mile team finished, having had to swim across the East Okement River, soaked and shivering, but proud of themselves and rightly so.

I expect that there were many times when the girls wanted to be anywhere other than the wild Moor, and maybe 'wished me, and all training, further', but many have continued with their walking, back-packing in different parts of the world. Some have returned to help with new Maynard teams, and there is no doubt that this experience produces leaders in all walks of life. Many also return to Dartmoor – there seems to be a love-hate relationship with it!

I have deliberately not mentioned anyone by name, as that is a slippery slope into forgetting someone! Suffice to say that I had a wonderful band of helpers from staff, parents and friends, who tirelessly gave up many weekends, and without whom I could never have managed. A very big thank you to all of them. They know who they are! Also a very big thank you to all the girls who taught me as much as I (hopefully), taught them! – for their companionship, laughter, tears, friendship and for putting up with every sort of discomfort with good humour and determination.

In 2006 I took part in 'The Abbots Way Walk', together with my daughter-in-law (the leader of the first ever Maynard Ten Tors team), and, being painfully aware of Anno Domini, felt like asking the question which one of the 1989 Maynard team had on their sweatshirt: 'Why can't Dartmoor be flat?'!

*In 2007, after Pat Read had written this, Ten Tors was stopped once again, due to truly atrocious weather conditions which were considered too dangerous to allow the participants to continue. Since Pat's handing over of the 'baton', Ten Tors has continued to go from strength to strength thanks to the unwavering commitment of Mrs Odile Saunders (Head of French), and her husband, Paul.

Ten Tors (A Pupil's View)

Sarah Moffat 1993–2003

I participated in Ten Tors in both 2000 (35-miles), and 2002 (45-miles), and enough time has now gone by that I can look back and focus on the good parts, and not the pain, etc.

35-mile team, Ten Tors 2000

The Ten Tors Challenge came into being in 1959 and has developed since then into an event which involves 2,400 young people every year, with intense competition to be one of the few selected to take part. In 1999, nearly half of my year group (30 girls), started the training that would lead 12 of us to the Ten Tors Event on Dartmoor in May 2000. We suffered through training weekends which varied from driving rain to freezing cold to blazing sunshine – the highlight being camping on Dartmoor in temperatures which apparently dropped to -10°C! During the months of training we learnt how not to get hopelessly lost (thanks to Colonel Sharpe who managed to find us no matter how far off course we were!), how to pitch tents in wind and rain, and how important food is to keeping cheerful.

The event itself in 2000 was certainly a challenge that we weren't fully prepared for. Ten Tors is known for its unpredictable and often extreme weather and in 2000 we were treated to one of the hottest weekends the event has seen. The heat made the already difficult route even more challenging and whilst sunny weather was preferable to the pouring rain seen in other years it brought with it its own dangers as a large number of participants were forced to retire suffering from the effects of dehydration and heat stroke. Our group successfully

Mrs Read, bottom left, with her 1989 Ten Tors groups.

completed the route thanks to some good teamwork and made it back to Okehampton in plenty of time to receive our medals and ensure that our spectacular sunburn was caught in photos as a reminder never to wear shorts and gaiters together again!

Ten Tors in 2002 attracted even more people than normal as the 2001 event had been cancelled because of the Foot and Mouth outbreak. The training followed much the same pattern as it had done two years previously but mysteriously it seemed much easier despite the fact we were covering greater distances – maybe our bodies had accustomed themselves to the abuse we were subjecting them to?! That year a number of us suffered recurrent injuries – problems with ankles and knees which added an extra dimension to the challenge. Even though a lot of us had completed the 35-mile route in 2000 it did not prevent us from getting horrifically lost all over again during training – in our defence the weather was atrocious with fog making it almost impossible to navigate. But this time it was Mr Saunders who had to come to our rescue.

Even though a lot of us had completed the 35-mile route in 2000 it did not prevent us from getting horrifically lost all over again during training – in our defence the weather was atrocious with fog making it almost impossible to navigate.

In May 2002 six of us set off on the 45-mile route across Dartmoor but only five were to complete the event this time. The weather this year was not as kind to us and it rained for the majority of the first day which made an already testing route much worse. Between the third and fourth Tors I was unfortunate/stupid enough to sprain my ankle (one of those irritating recurrent injuries I mentioned), and although the rest of the team helped me by carrying some of my kit, by the time we reached the fifth Tor at 7.30pm that evening it was clear that I would not be able to complete the event. It is upsetting for any Ten Tors team to have a member drop out part way round – after training together for months there is a 'we're going to finish this together' attitude, but it happens to many teams each year. It took the army over four hours to get me back to Okehampton by foot, 4 x 4 vehicle and minibus, and once there I decided that rather than going home I would wait for the following day and watch the rest of the team come in. The other five members of the team completed the event at 2pm and it was hard seeing them coming over the hills bearing the pink balloons we had carried with us as I should have been there with them!

Ten Tors is an experience that will live with the participants for the rest of their lives – the elation, the despair, the exhaustion, and, for me, the knowledge that Dartmoor defeated me in 2002.

The Duke of Edinburgh's Award

Sarah Moffat 1993–2003

The mission statement of this award provides as good an introduction as I could think of: 'The Duke of Edinburgh's Award is committed to providing for young people an enjoyable, challenging and rewarding programme of personal development, which is of the highest quality and the widest reach.'

The Duke of Edinburgh's Award began in 1956 and since then around three million young people have taken up the challenge. Participants can start at one of three levels: Bronze, Silver and Gold; and many go on to complete all three levels. In 2005/06, 40,332 young people gained a Bronze Award, 14,667 gained a Silver Award and 6,256 gained a Gold Award. So whilst the Award has seen an increased number of young people participating in it, the achievement of the Gold Award is still relatively rare and something to be truly proud of.

I would recommend the Duke of Edinburgh's Award to any young person who wants to challenge themselves, meet people, gain new skills, and improve their CV!

At Bronze and Silver level the Award consists of four sections: Service, Expedition, Physical Recreation, and Skills. At Gold level there is an additional Residential Project which involves spending at least five days away from home with other Award participants.

I began my Bronze Award when I was in Lower 5 in 1999. At this time the only way to gain the necessary training to complete the Expedition section of the Award was to train with those students hoping to take part in Ten Tors that year. There were no organised expeditions or training sessions available and at Bronze, Silver and Gold levels I joined other groups in order to complete my expeditions. As a result I believe that I am the only person from my year group to have completed all three levels of the Award.

Things have changed a lot in the years since then and the Duke of Edinburgh's Award is being run very successfully at the Maynard due to the dedication of certain members of staff, most recently Mrs Thorne, Mrs Roche, Dr Burgess and Dr Rudling. I returned to the School in the summers of 2004 and 2005 to help supervise large numbers of Bronze and Silver participants on their expeditions and I was pleased to see how popular the Award had become! Long may it continue!

Participating in the Duke of Edinburgh's Award has had a real impact on me in the last 10 years. I have gained skills that will be useful in the future; met many new friends who I am still in contact with; achieved something that few others do and which stands out on my CV; pushed myself to complete something which, on occasion, seemed impossible; and gained a level of self-sufficiency and self-confidence that will stand me in good stead.

I would recommend the Duke of Edinburgh's Award to any young person who wants to challenge themselves, meet people, gain new skills, and improve their CV! And to all those over-25s out there – you may be too old to complete the Award yourself but you can get involved too by helping a local Award group!

A 2008 Gold winner! Rosamond Luther with Mrs Thorne at a County Hall presentation in recognition of Devon participants collecting Gold awards

1889–1891

Jane Taunton, from an interview with Doris Bradbeer and Peggy Gilpin (Andrews), in 1970

So it came about that Doris Bradbeer and I visited Miss Taunton: a surprising experience for me as – expecting to see a Really Old Lady – I met a slim, upright, smartly-dressed little lady with a lively face and beautiful hair expertly styled, whose age one would have guessed to be a youthful 70 [she was 97!].

Miss Taunton's father had adopted the Army as a career, travelling out to join his regiment, the 50th Queen's Own, during the Maori War. He came to love New Zealand and Australia, but it was later, when stationed at Topsham Barracks in Exeter, that he met and married the daughter of Mr and Mrs Boughton Kyngdon, members of a well-known Exeter family. It was this connection that brought Major Taunton and his family back to Exeter for a year's leave in 1889, and it was then that Miss Taunton (aged 16) went to the Exeter High School for Girls. Her parents had taken a house in York Road, and she went daily, unaccompanied, to school. Later on, being in the Upper Form, she was only required to attend in the mornings from 9.15 am to 1.15 pm, except for some special subjects. She said that 'in my day, Exeter was a very quiet dreamy old town – I can't even remember trams!'

At this time Miss Hall was Headmistress. Miss Taunton remembers her as a short, very plump lady, an excellent Headmistress and a wonderful organiser. Among the form mistresses were Miss Powell and Miss Turner, a small charming woman of whom she was particularly fond, and who succeeded Miss Hall as headmistress. After morning roll-call in the hall, the girls took part in a graceful 'pretty' form of gymnastics, using balls, clubs and bells, and frequently watched by visitors. The young Jane Taunton did so well in her studies that it was suggested that she might stay on at school for a second year to take the Senior Cambridge examination, and this she did. When her family returned to Australia she was placed in the care of the Misses Templar, two pleasant ladies, cousins of Sir John Kennaway. They lived in Dix's Field and – loving youthful society – sometimes welcomed into their home girls whose parents were abroad. Miss Taunton recalls their concern for her welfare: when she set off to take her examination they insisted that she should carry a small hot-water bottle in her muff! She remembers too that: 'When Miss Templar took me to a picnic in the woods at Sir John Kennaway's place [Escot, Ottery St Mary] we went in a kind of wagonette, and his elderly aunt Miss Augusta Kennaway met us with a serving man laden with food. Afterwards she took us over the house. On Sundays, she told us, no games were allowed – a very strict regime – all toys having been put away on Saturday nights! On Sundays I was taken to service in Exeter Cathedral.'

Among her school-fellows Miss Taunton remembers Nellie Tillard. She frequently visited Colonel Tillard's family at Kenton, and says that 'When I spent the week-end with my friend Nellie Tillard a smart dog-cart with a man in livery and cockade came to fetch us'. Nellie was a girl of great character; she longed to become a doctor, but this being impossible trained as a nurse, and later became a dedicated Christian Scientist. She was also a militant suffragette and a vigorous follower of Mrs Pankhurst, participating to the full in the movement even to the point of chaining herself to railings and being arrested and imprisoned. Years later Nellie visited Australia to inspect the condition of prisons there, and she and Miss Taunton met again in New South Wales.

Miss Taunton was successful in her Senior Cambridge examination, passing in French, History, Geography, Arithmetic, Divinity (which was taught in the School by the Archdeacon of Exeter), and in English Language and Literature in which she obtained Honours. She left school in 1891 and returned to Australia. Here she undertook the education of her brothers and sisters – there were 13 children in the family, though three died in childhood.

Later she taught with marked success in leading Australian schools – Ascham School in Sydney and Toorak College in Melbourne. After some years she accepted more personal teaching posts, and went as governess to one of the stations in Southern Australia, situated in an isolated position with vast tracts of land supporting as many as 90,000 sheep.

(In 1973, Jane celebrated her 100th birthday with a tea party in Ryan House; she lived to be 103.)

1907–1918

Mary Prees-Thomas (Hamlin)

Taken from accounts written for and published in the 1984/85 and 1985/86 school magazines

Mary Hamlin, as she was known professionally, had a distinguished career during the 1930s, 40s and 50s as a concert singer, both live and broadcast. At the age of 60 she became a Professor and Examiner at the Royal Academy of Music. In 1935 she returned to the Maynard to perform in the School Hall.

I first trod the paths of the Exeter High School (The Maynard later) in September 1907. It was my first and only school. In those days it was just a school with a long drive up to its doors for carriages – no Fives Court, no netball or tennis courts except two in the upper garden facing Spicer Road. Traceyville next door belonged to my great-aunt and her sister. There was no large cookery room – only a small classroom [the Physics lab in the mid-80s] leading by a passage to the Hall, which had rib-stalls on the walls, and a large stained-glass window with portraits of great poets, at which one gazed during daily Prayers or during a boring Prize Giving.

The school encouraged me to be myself, to aim high, to use my talents as a service of joy to my fellow men by singing and playing the piano; also I could compose music, one piece being a march for taking classes out of Prayers twice a week. During the 1914–18 war, our Head, Miss Trenerry, gave permission for me to sing and play after school hours at the many hospitals for wounded soldiers in Exeter, to make Red Cross supplies, and, instead of moving into the Sixth Form, to join five other girls in the tiny Cookery School, a room that led back-stage on to the Hall platform. Here Miss Haldane or Miss Wigley tried to teach us to make the war-time marmalade of carrots plus one orange, cakes with dried-egg powder and macaroni cheese. We made very nice soups, maize bread and rolled and curled margarine; we also provided suppers for the poor staff who suffered under our feeble menus. We cooked at one oven, the door of which was frequently opened, but Miss Wigley was a trooper when teaching us laundry work (you pronounced it 'landry'), with no electric aids at all. I forget what we washed, but I don't think our housewifery class (pronounced 'husifery') yielded very clean results. However, we did learn how to iron, with irons dashed to the top of the cookery rings, seeing who could get there first.

Kindergarten pupils, c1906

Maths and Games were not 'my line' but Music, Scripture, Botany, Nature Study and Languages were. Because I was constantly the winner for the solo singing prize given by Dr Wood [Music Master] I had to sing a song before the Board of Governors on Prize Distribution Day. When I was about 13 I took up Wood Carving, introduced to school by Miss Banmann, and learned to carve a cover for a photo box in oak. Carving was taught by a young man called Pook, who belonged to the famous carving firm in Exeter, Harry Hems. Dancing I did with a certain very elderly lady who had classes at the Rougement Hotel; in addition, to stimulate musicianship, I joined the school's weekly class of Dalcroze Eurythmics. We had to dance barefoot in a black crêpe chemise, making movements of body and expression to music and marking our rhythm to different tunes played on the piano. It was very cold in winter, and we learned to express fear, pleasure, butterflies, and stormy petrels with faces, arms and hands, and to fling our bodies to music in transports of joy, as well as cringing in deadly poses.

They wanted me to train as a teacher, but it was too limiting for me with a good voice and talents for piano and music sight-reading. Eventually, in 1918, I left and went to the Royal Academy of Music. It's a joy to me to know how the School has extended, prospered and continued to be a first-rate girls' school – no boys to plague you! (We met our boys outside school, with coffee at Deller's Café on Saturday mornings and moonlight flittings in various large green fields after homework.)

The Maynard made me a healthy worker, gave me ideals and high aims, and although not bookishly clever, I love books. My report seldom said anything beyond 'Mary is conscientious', which I found counts, because it means you listen for the still, small voice within you and follow your star. Three cheers for the Maynard, long may she flourish and have dedicated teachers!

c1890

Gertrude McCrea (as recalled in 1969)

Third Form, 1892. Standing, L–R: Lorna Bellow, Olive Tosswill, May Puttick, Amelia Sheffield, Hilda McCrea (another sister of Gertrude's?), Bella Roe. Seated, L–R: Dorothy Rundle, Winnie Edmonds, Miss Sellick, Elsie Horswell, Jessie Hucklebridge. Miss Sellick was their Form Mistress and also taught Classics.

There was no Exeter High School when I was born [1876], and I can well remember often being taken with my sister Margaret [12 months' younger], by our nurse from our home in Magdalen Street round the corner to the Barn Fields, where on little field paths we would toddle along together without falling on to the pavement. As time went on the field disappeared and the High School took its place. Margaret and I were first educated in a private school but later on we went to the Exeter High School. Miss Hall was Head Mistress and her portrait hung in the hall. She wore a white cap.

Gertrude's name is one of the earliest on the University Honours Board in the School Hall: '1898 Classical Tripos, Class III Newnham College'. She became headmistress of Stafford Girls' High School from about 1910 to 1946. A fellow Maynardian, Miss Cummin, taught History there at the same time.

1912–1922

Frances & Amy Clogg

By kind permission of Amy's daughter, Dr Shirley Whittard

Frances left the Maynard to go to Cheltenham, partly to be away as her father became increasingly ill with cancer of the larynx, but had to return home after a year to help support her mother. Amy, being four years younger, was not as cognisant of what was happening, and took refuge in school life to help her cope with her father's illness and death when she was 14. The following is taken from Amy's diary.

'During these years I was deeply involved in school life, work and play. Besides games afternoons there were always matches on Saturdays, home or away: Tennis, Cricket, Netball and sometimes Lacrosse; also gym displays, dancing displays and school plays. In the Upper V we took the Senior Oxford exam with matric exemption (1920), Maynard scholarship and Newnham scholarship 1921. Then came the terrible day when I turned up for the Zoology practical at the end of London Inter. in the afternoon instead of the morning. This meant I had not got exemption from London 1st Medical (a necessity for Newnham), but our Science mistress, Miss Burne, an old Newnhamite herself, pleaded my cause to such effect that I was allowed to go up and take Cambridge 1st Medical (recently opened to women at the end of my first term).

The last couple of years at the Maynard had been a time of increasing responsibility as a junior prefect and then as Head Girl. Miss Trenerry, our Head Mistress, an autocrat of the old school, suddenly resigned to get married, and was succeeded by Miss Dixon who was all for self-government by the girls and school rules to be drawn up and administered by the prefects. This made life difficult as we had not been brought up that way.

Frances had taken shorthand and typing courses when she came home from Cheltenham. She was always of a literary mind and had got 1st class honours in the Senior Oxford exam in 1916 when she was in her last term at the Maynard. She worked as a part-time secretary to the vicar of St David's, and then to Miss Dixon [Headmistress] at the Maynard, but she was not keen on it and persuaded Mother it would be more cheerful to move to London when I left school.'

1930s & 1940s

Jocelyn Hemming (Foulkes) and her sisters, Barbara Cork & Nancy Thurley

After a mercifully short period in the kindergarten at St Margaret's (during which I was a bored five-year-old making houses out of matchsticks), my elder sister and I entered Traceyville in late 1929 or early 1930. I recall little about Traceyville except that there were boys in the class, Murray French being the one I best remember. Everything was on a small scale: mini tables and chairs and mini loos. This struck me as odd as we didn't have anything like that at home. I think our ambition was to get into The Big School – into the Lower First, and I suppose this happened at about the age of seven. By this time our younger sister had arrived at Traceyville. The Headmistress was then Miss Dixon, but she retired and was succeeded by Miss Ryan who had been Science teacher at Cheltenham Ladies College.

As juniors we played Rounders on the lawn opposite Tregear and Netball on the lower tennis courts in winter. We played Hockey several times a week in winter and Cricket in summer on the fields in Barrack Road, where the present Royal Devon & Exeter Hospital was built, and had matches against other schools on Saturdays. Prayers were held in the Hall at 9am and we all stood in lines to sing hymns or sat cross-legged on the floor while one of the prefects read the Lesson of the day. When I reached the dizzy heights of being a prefect myself I remember an occasion when Joyce Bowden was reading from the gospel of St John. We knew she had a boyfriend called John and of course did our best to embarrass her when she had to read out in front of the whole school, 'There was a man called from God whose name was John'. She was pretty cross about that afterwards. I had a Cornish friend called Pauline Roskilly. We always tried to stand next to each other at prayers and sing the hymns in Cornish or Devon accents and sometimes substituted the original words for what we considered more meaningful – like 'slapdown' for 'prostrate' and so on. We were never found out because we were standing in the middle of the Hall and all the staff were at the back.

1st VII Netball team, 1939/40

We spent our mid-morning breaks doing what schoolchildren have always done – 'mucking about' with friends by the Fives Court, playing with yo-yos which were a tremendous craze in about 1935, and sucking aniseed balls which changed colour in your mouth. School lunch was very good and, for those days, extremely healthy. There were always huge bowls of salad, fruit and veg all mixed up together. Prunes and custard of course. Once I was sitting at the head of a table and decided to show my friends how chickens drank water. One of the staff saw me messing about and I was sent out of the dining room to stand in the corridor until lunch was over! I don't remember other punishments except once as a very small junior I was caught running in the corridor and was sent to the Prefects' Room. There I was handed a copy of *Hereward the Wake* and told to read the first paragraph out loud in front of all the prefects. I was terrified, and of course they all laughed at my stumbling efforts!

Music and drama were not particularly well covered. The music mistress, Miss Alcock, belonged to the 'thumping the piano' school and seemed always in a furious temper about something or other. The Cathedral organist, Dr Alfred Wilcock, also gave singing lessons – an unrewarding task as I remember. Poor man, he used to sigh despairingly at our efforts to sing in tune. Because of his name we called him 'Burnt Cakes'. In spite of all, however, the School did put on one or two quite good musical and theatrical events before the war, Humperdinck's *Hansel and Gretel* being the most ambitious, and the staff wrote and acted their own spoof musical *What Katy Did* – which I remember as being great entertainment. It was always extremely amusing to see the normally serious-minded teachers letting down their hair!

I was 15 when the Second World War broke out. It must have been an enormous worry for the Head and staff. We had regular air raid drill and had to carry our gas masks everywhere. Quite early in the war we were told of the sinking of HMS Exeter in the South Atlantic. The ship's chaplain came from Exeter Cathedral and was reported to have gone down with the ship. We were all marched to the Cathedral for a memorial service, but it later turned out that many of the crew had been saved, among them the chaplain.

By 1941 I was in the Sixth Form and preparing for Oxford Entrance and Higher Certificate (more or less the equivalent of A-levels today.) I remember that a Miss Pettifer, who taught us French in the Upper Sixth, had a brother who was killed in the unsuccessful commando raid on Dieppe, a tragic event which was all too often repeated in our community. At the same time one of the Sixth Formers (Priscilla Riley), got engaged to a soldier, and we all had to admire her diamond engagement ring, which surprisingly she was allowed to wear while at school – the wearing of jewellery other than watches being absolutely forbidden! It was decided that the seniors should do fire-watching duties overnight in the School and a rota was set up. There was only a handful of us in the Sixth Form so our time for duty came round quite often. We took it in turns to sleep in our clothes in a camp bed in the Remedial Room and then patrol the grounds at night with a member of staff. We were trained to use a stirrup pump in a bucket of water for putting out incendiary bombs. I cannot imagine that we would have been of the slightest use if the School had caught on fire! Eventually of course it happened – in May 1942. It was a weekend just before the beginning of term and none of the girls was on fire duty that night.

Watching the city burning from the top floor of our house out at Alphington is a sight I shall never forget. My parents who were both doctors had left for the hospital at about 4am, on foot, as the roads were impassable. I got on my bike after breakfast and picked up a friend who lived in Exwick. Parts of St Thomas had been badly hit, telephone lines were down everywhere and there were fire hoses criss-crossing the streets so riding a bike was difficult. The centre of Exeter was a heap of rubble and half of Southernhay had gone. We got to the Maynard eventually and found that five bombs had landed in various parts of the building and grounds and the library was in ruins. I think we spent the next few days helping to sort out the books that remained in the rubble, but any hope that school would be postponed was soon dashed and in no time we were all allocated places at Exeter, Hele's, and Bishop Blackall Schools. The Maynard boarding house in Summerlands had been completely destroyed and accommodation had to be found for many of the girls who came from a long way off. I went to Hele's School for the rest of the summer term and did all my exams there and got a place at St Hugh's College, Oxford to read Geography. I left the Maynard in July 1942 after 13 perfectly happy years.

Domestic Science class, c1930s

My elder sister, Barbara, had left school aged 16 in 1939 to join the Land Army. Not academically inclined, she excelled at gymnastics and all games, won many 'colours' and was awarded the coveted 'carriage girdle' for good deportment – this was a distinctive blue/grey girdle worn with our tunics instead of the ordinary black ones. There were not many of these given out, and it was considered quite an honour. She also did Domestic Science under Miss Baker who taught cooking, ironing and washing clothes. One of the more unpleasant chores they did in Domestic Science was to clean the lavatories at Tregear (there must have been a domestic staff shortage!). When I was in the Sixth Form Miss Ryan decided that those who were doing purely academic subjects should also know how to cook, making do out of our meagre wartime rations. So once a week we had to bring our own materials and were taught pastry making. I got ticked off for not using up every bit of the cooking apples I had brought from home. We were allowed to take our culinary efforts home and I seem to remember my 'herb pie' didn't go down too well with the family!

Nancy, my younger sister, and always a rebel, had gone away to boarding school in Salisbury in 1938 but was brought back to the Maynard, much against her wishes, in 1940 when the invasion of Britain seemed imminent. She says that the best part of becoming a senior was having the job of ringing the bell between lessons, because it meant leaving class two minutes before the end! But by the middle of the summer term of 1944 she decided she had had enough of the Maynard School and during one lunch hour she walked into Exeter to the Recruiting Office at the Castle and signed on to join the WRNS. She lied about her age, because she was not old enough to volunteer, and when the Head found out she promptly expelled her!

1935–1940

Clare Murley (Hodges)

I started at the Maynard School at the age of 11 at the same time as the new Head, Miss Ryan, was appointed. She followed Miss Dixon who had suffered a long period of ill-health. The school had lacked direction for a long time but the pupils benefited from the positive feeling that followed with the arrival of Miss Ryan who brought with her a friendly and yet authoritative approach. I think that some members of staff were newly recruited. We loved our teacher of English who was Miss Lane, a favourite with a succession of girls; Miss Evans made Science interesting as did Miss Elcombe in Geography. I cannot remember the name of the teacher who introduced us to Early History in my first year but she seemed to be a gentle lady in her approach to us. Miss Cartwright (later Mrs Bennett), the new member of staff for History, came as a surprise as she towered, head and shoulders in height, over everybody. With her teaching us, History lessons became even more interesting with a pattern of two weekly schedules and an opportunity to produce our own contributions in photos or text that enhanced the project. When we reached the period before and after the Second World War that brought so many changes in the life of women, she impressed on us that we needed to learn from it and to become good citizens. She said that we should also remember the people who had struggled over those years before being able to eventually bring about changes in the attitude of both politicians and the general public. Miss Anderson was the Classics mistress and Deputy Headmistress. I needed Latin for a career in Pharmacy and used to have private tutoring in Miss Anderson's flat at Barnfield Crescent. This was at the top of Barnfield Road on my daily route to school after I left the bus at the city centre. It is now quite a different approach to the school buildings as a busy road [Western Way] divides it half way down the hill.

Miss Elcombe and Miss Hebditch

In subjects, I found that in my form I was on the same level as the others except in French. Those girls who had been in Traceyville, as younger pupils at the school, had already studied the language. Most of the time I made good progress with my average marks maintaining a level around the middle of the rest in the form. Occasionally I would surprise everyone, including myself, with a top-of-form result – however my results in Art were very low. I was very sensitive to teacher Miss Barker's sarcastic comments and I felt that I had no ability. In spite of this, in later life, in my hobbies of flower arranging and embroidery design I was very successful. Miss Alcock, who composed the music for the School Song, was the Music mistress of my era. I remember she became very exasperated with the whole school one day. Everyone was assembled to practise for a special occasion and when we did not get a seven-fold 'Amen' correct (or something equally important!), after many tries she gave us all the punishment of an Order Mark each. Even at that age I somehow thought that this was a rather negative thing to do.

We loved our teacher of English who was Miss Lane, a favourite with a succession of girls; Miss Evans made Science interesting as did Miss Elcombe in Geography.

At some stage Miss Ryan and my mother decided that my confidence needed boosting so I attended the Drama Class after school for one term. I did not go back the next term so the experiment obviously did not work. I remember a production of *Hansel and Gretel* in the late 1930s. I was very impressed by the imaginative use of ordinary equipment, such as the heavy forms we used in the Gym, and the transformation from stage to a woodland scene.

For three years, because of my tendency to have rheumatism, in our Gym period I only did the drill during the first half then I was allowed to sit out on the steps of the platform and watch the rest of the girls swing on ropes, climb the parallel bars and leap over the apparatus. I was secretly pleased to watch as any great physical exercise left me not only stiff but suffering with painful joints for several days. I enjoyed Netball on a court in the school grounds but for Hockey we had to walk quite a distance to the playing field and after a busy session running up and down in the game and two journeys in the bus to get home, I was always extremely tired. Today, medically, there is the understanding that modern facilities such as showers on

Cast of the 1938 production of *Hansel & Gretel*

site would have helped me had they been available. However I seemed to accept having the difficulties and remember on occasions just patiently going up the main steps by the Hall one by one. When sitting-out during Gym I had time to gaze around the Hall while others were getting their exercise. I was drawn to the list on the wall of the great achievers of earlier years on an Honours Board. I can only remember one girl's name – Mabel Reeks. I felt sorry for her as I felt that she must have suffered a great deal of teasing.

I looked up to the prefects and senior girls and admired those splendid ones with pale blue 'carriage girdles' – a couple of them had thick ropes of plaited hair hanging down their straight backs; they always seemed to me to be so very important. Many members of my own form were good in a variety of subjects. I remember in those days all the girls in my form being very friendly and there seemed no evidence of bullying.

I left the Maynard at the age of 16 after passing School Certificate with Exemption from Matriculation and was therefore able to start my training in Pharmacy.

My daughter once lived in Norfolk with her family and on a visit to Blickling Hall I was surprised and delighted to see Sir John Maynard with other courtiers in a very large painting in one of the rooms. The familiar Maynard coat of arms was also there.

I have always appreciated the good basic education that I received and a realisation of my own capabilities meant that I was able to make the most of my various experiences in life. I was a Magistrate in the Waterside and New Forest area for 25 years and was always conscious of the School motto 'to keep the right hand dealing'!

1936–1942

Professor Dame Margaret Turner Warwick (Harvey Moore)
DM (Oxon), PhD (Lond), FRCP, FAcad.Med.Sci.

I joined the Maynard just over 70 years ago (1936) at the age of 12. I had started school at the City of London School for Girls but my older sisters and I were all beleaguered by middle ear infections and recurrent pneumonia – in the days before antibiotics. We therefore moved to the country in Kent and attended Walthamstow Hall School for Girls which was a disaster. I was put into a form above my age and completely failed to cope with the work. I felt isolated and hated the school anyway. In fact I was also seriously deaf but as with so many children, the only manifestation was poor performance – only later after we had moved again, was my deafness diagnosed and responded dramatically to treatment. I was astonished to find how much I had been missing.

My father was a barrister and used to follow the judges down to the West Country on the Western Circuit. He decided to move us all back to his beloved Devon and as he said 'then all the circuit judges can come to me'. We lived up on the hill at 5 Pennsylvania Park, before they were converted into flats. Each of these marvellous Regency houses was a family home. We had a lovely garden at the back and a communal garden in the front for hockey in winter and tennis in the summer. I and my three sisters walked to and from school which took about half an hour each way. We could have taken the bus part of the way but we preferred to walk.

I joined the Maynard in the middle of the summer term. Wisely I was put into a lower class than my age – 3A I think – because I had missed so much time through sickness at my previous schools. However I was promised that I could move up a class if I got more than an average of eight and a half out of 10 marks on each weekly assessment over the first half of the autumn term. With a huge effort I succeeded. The school, in consultation with my parents but not with me, then said that because I was doing so well, it would be much better to stay down in the same class. I was bitterly disappointed and felt very let down but I was determined never in the future to get a weekly average mark below eight and a half just to show them what I thought! I am sure that in the event the School was right but I thought it was a rather mean way to behave! In those days children were not consulted or even given explanations. However, it certainly taught me how to work.

A very happy bonus for 'staying down' was that I met Jane Pinsent who became a lifelong close friend. Now at 83 years of age we are still in touch. She was both clever and talented. She went up to Cambridge and became a research Microbiologist. She married Quentin Gibson FRS when he was Professor of Biochemistry at Sheffield University, and he is now an international haemoglobinologist. They moved to the USA and have both done brilliantly. At the Maynard Jane and I both volunteered to be lab girls, putting out the chemistry apparatus before classes began. This taught us a lot of Chemistry and also gave us an excuse not to attend school prayers – until Miss Clissold, Head of Chemistry, rumbled us. The school had no problem with multiple faiths and there was no question of attempting to modify school prayers to accommodate these. It was simply accepted with respect that the Jewish children had their own prayers separately but would rejoin the school assembly afterwards for announcements, reporting of school marks and so on.

Miss Clissold in rehearsal for a school production, 1942. Note, in the background, the bomb damage to the north end of the main building already being repaired.

Standards of good, helpful and proper behaviour were encouraged by a very simple but effective device. In place of the standard dark blue 'string' that everyone wore with their school tunics, a small number of elegant, broad, pale blue 'carriage girdles' were given at the end of each term for deportment and good behaviour. These were much sought after and they could be withdrawn if a girl's standard lapsed. The psychology was a simple, subtle and very effective inducement to encourage all those old-fashioned standards of good behaviour, courtesy and consideration, combined with deportment, without having to use heavy-handed Victorian methods. There was an occasion (I remember the names but will not mention them!), when two girls in my form were found rolling on the floor fighting during 'break'. A member of staff instantly and silently removed both their carriage girdles – no arguments, no investigation, no moral lectures. Both girls were mortified. Both got their girdles back again a term or two later. I suppose the system had to be abandoned when the school uniform changed. What a pity. I wonder if anything as effective has replaced them.

Staff photograph late 1920s/early 30s. Miss Hartley is in this photograph, possibly far left in the back row, with Miss Dixon, Headmistress, centre.

We had some wonderful teachers. I remember Miss Hartley who taught Maths. She was quiet and gentle but very encouraging. She expected children to share her enthusiasm for solving mathematical problems. She did not mind how you got there so long as the answer to the sum was right. However she explained without any implied criticism, that the more steps one took the greater the chances of making a mistake and that therefore the fun and safety of Maths was to solve the problem using the shortest route. This made it very exciting. Miss Evans was Head of Biology and was much liked and trusted by everyone. When she retired she moved to Ealing and many of us continued to visit her there. Miss Ryan (a physicist) had recently been appointed Headmistress in 1935 and I remember the incredulity of the School that a scientist had been considered suitable for a headship. Why as schoolgirls we understood that this was rather unusual at that time, I am not sure, but we felt rather proud to be part of a new and very modern development. Likewise I remember an equal feeling of being ahead of the times when Miss Cartwright (History) married Mr Bennett, the Vicar of Alphington, and was still allowed to continue teaching. Miss Anderson taught Latin and was completely uninhibited in voicing her disapproval of how English grammar was taught, or in her view rather not taught, in the school. These were the days when the new method of colour parsing was favoured – green for a verb, red for a noun, yellow for an adjective. She therefore made it her business to teach us proper English grammar her way, with none of this colour nonsense, before we could understand how to write Latin. After the major summer School Certificate examinations were finished, and rather than letting us waste good school time to the end of term (which still seems to happen in some schools), she abandoned Latin and settled us down immediately on a crash course of Greek, just as a treat.

I remember the incredulity of the School that a scientist [Miss Ryan] had been considered suitable for a headship.

Most of the school lessons were straightforward academic subjects. They were taught thoroughly although not in any particularly innovative way – apart of course from the attempt at colour parsing! We took lessons seriously because it was expected. Each piece of class work and homework in every subject was marked out of 10 and the overall average given as the weekly mark. The results for each child in every form were read out each week before the whole school. I don't know how others felt but I found this quite stressful, but regarded it more as a challenge rather than a question of 'mark grubbing'. On the whole I think the system was helpful (although I believe that the very public way in which they were read out was very hard on lesser achievers). At least we were all very clear where we stood. I often hear from my grandchildren that they wish they knew more clearly how their teachers viewed their performance. Today there may be so much care taken to protect children from disappointment that they are left with considerable uncertainty about how they are doing – encouragement is of course vital but more is needed, especially at a more senior level.

I do not remember many activities run by the School after the standard day. There was a small choir but it did not do much. We also had some current affairs lectures. One was given by Mr Henry Michelmore, a partner in the famous family firm of solicitors in Exeter, who had distinguished himself in the First World War, and who was very keen on the peace-keeping work of the United Nations. At the age of about 13 I was asked to give the vote of thanks – I learnt it by heart and it must have been dreadful.

Sport was strong at the Maynard. I particularly enjoyed Netball and Hockey. My Tennis was less good. However, when I was about 15 I managed to get into the final eight in a whole school competition. This happened because I managed to beat a member of the school's first team by lobbing so relentlessly (it was the only stroke I had), that it made her very cross and she lost her concentration. When I moved on to St Paul's Girls' School in London I was asked to show them how to play Cricket which had been part of the Maynard curriculum since the early 1900s.

I think the 1930s was a good time to be at school. My sisters and I all intended to go up to university which was already becoming more feasible for women. We all did so, largely thanks to the thorough grounding at the Maynard. Life was stable, the national financial depression was over and the imminence of the Second World War had not percolated through to children so life was relatively simple and altogether pretty straightforward. There was no television or computer games as time-wasting distractions; there was no 'rat race' of competitive formal after-school activities and, for better or for worse, no fixation on socializing by mobile phone. 'Teenagers' had not been invented! My sisters and I all learned the piano in a pretty relaxed way and I went to Philharmonic subscription concerts at the Rougemont Hotel which began my lifelong love of the violin. For the rest it was up to families not school to broaden one's education. In our household at least, the motto was creativity without competition. Fortunately mother provided this in full measure, introducing us to all manner of creative arts and crafts – watercolour painting, plaster of Paris sculpture, pewter and leatherwork, lino and wood cuts, dressmaking, knitting complex patterns, crochet, tatting, and much more besides. We went camping as a family in the summer, we rode ponies at the local stable and joined the Cathedral Girl Guides company because it was regarded as good to mix with children from other schools and backgrounds.

None of this was regarded as a responsibility of the school. Although in our family money was reasonably tight and mostly spent on our education we were very privileged to have parents who gave us so many opportunities. So much so, that the four of us formed a pretty self-contained tribe.

There are other trivial, mostly happy, memories of School:

My spelling was (and still is) poor. Quite early on I found that I could disguise this pretty well with poor hand writing. As a result I was sent to a special writing class. This was a problem because I obviously could not afford to improve. At the end of term I had managed to make so little progress that, much to my relief, I was discharged from the class in ignominy. It would, of course, have been better to have made me take more care of my spelling rather than my writing. Spell check looks after me now.

Two other memories concern food. There was a selection of buns at 'break'. The jam doughnuts were much the best but one was rarely far enough up the queue to get one so a plain currant bun had to do. Another surprising memory was that the school cabbage was some of the best I have ever tasted – very green and sweet and not overcooked. I wish I knew the variety and how they managed to serve it so well. We sat down to a proper two-course hot lunch served in the Domestic Science room but temporarily converted into a dining room each day for the purpose. It was a sociable, orderly affair.

Another surprising memory was that the school cabbage was some of the best I have ever tasted – very green and sweet and not overcooked.

On a more serious note, one of the most lasting memories of the war was when Exeter got bombed. The following morning we all dashed down to see if the School had been damaged which of course it had. However, within a matter of a few days we had been accommodated at Bishop Blackall School. Our partly-dissected dogfish had been retrieved from the rubble and we continued with our Biology lesson exactly where we had left off. The efficiency, collaboration and innovation between the teachers at both schools showed the dedication and determination of all the staff. This is one of the many unsung stories of the war.

In 1942, father had returned to the Bar in London because many of the younger barristers had been called up. The Battle of Britain was over and father said 'if we were going to be bombed in Exeter we might as well go back to London'. And so we did, just in time for the doodlebugs !

I will always be extremely grateful to the Maynard for giving me such a happy and disciplined start to life, teaching me the fascination of Science and the fun of learning. I knew I wanted to study Medicine from the age of eight and the School set me on my way. I had no idea that this start would lead to such a wonderful and fulfilling life.

1939–1944

Phyl Mullins (Hodges)

At 13 years old, in 1939, we were still children: we grew up during the six years of war. Miss Ryan and her team ensured we still benefited from the traditional Maynard education of scholarship and character building that runs like a thread from 1658 to the present day. This enormous challenge was met by them with imagination and a lot of common sense.

When I first started at Maynard, my idea of true happiness was a Latin-free day and being near enough to the front of the Buns 'n' Milk queue to bag a doughnut from Mrs Duckett. Late arrivals had to make do with 'carseats' (the name we gave to flat, tough, square, meagrely-fruited buns, with the consistency of a hard cushion!). In later years a good night's sleep had priority, as the wail of the air raid sirens prised us from our beds.

Shortages resulted in 'Make do and Mend'. My school tunic was not a flattering garment for a teenager on a high-carbohydrate diet so I decided to let down its meagre hem. Sadly there was daylight along the bottom edge so it had to come up rather than down! My route home was along Barrack Road and I had to run the gauntlet of whistling soldiers as I steered my bike, hung on to my boater and tried to keep my tunic down.

Group of older girls with staff, July 1943

Once, on holiday, I saw a Spanish ship loaded with onions and it reminded me of the excitement in school of buying a raffle ticket; first prize an onion. What a prize it would have been to take home to my mother! Money-raising was a way of life. Did we actually buy our own Spitfire? How many miles of bandages did we supply to the Red Cross? Was this a government ploy to reduce consumerism, I wonder? There was not much we could buy: there were few sweets, clothes were rationed, cosmetics like gold dust.

During my year in Upper 5, with Miss Lane as Form Mistress, we had the idea of sending a regular parcel through the Red Cross to a prisoner of war whose family could not afford to do so. His name was Tony and I seemed to be the one who wrote the letters to him and was responsible for sending the money – my biggest regret has been that I did not save his letters. They were about his interests in Civvy Street mainly, little about his imprisonment until he was on the infamous march between camps in bitter winter weather. He wrote about the soldiers who fell by the wayside and were left to die. These letters brought home the grim reality of war. There was money in hand when he was repatriated and my mother wrote to the Red Cross asking if it could be used to pay his rail fare for a visit. It was a strange meeting! We had exchanged so many letters. That weekend there was a ration of petrol issued for non-business use so we were able to take him on a tour of Dartmoor. My mother entertained him when I was at school and asked him how he would like to spend his last afternoon. His choice was to luxuriate in our bathroom! For hours! I wonder if it was not only the novelty of a bathroom he was enjoying but the fact that he was in charge of the key. When he left he thanked me for what we had done and said that he would have died without the parcels and the contact. He owed us nothing, the debt was ours to him and his fellow servicemen – I made that very clear! I wonder if his fellow prisoners knew that he was writing to a bunch of schoolgirls?

The Head Boy arrived with a message from the Headmaster: 'Dr. Andrews would like to squeeze you all in the Chapel at Assembly'. Miss Lane's kindly brown eyes twinkled as she graciously accepted the invitation.

Reorganisation of lessons after the School was bombed was undertaken with efficiency in an amazingly short time. Upper 5 assembled at Exeter School in a tizzy of excitement. The Head Boy arrived with a message from the Headmaster: 'Dr. Andrews would like to squeeze you all in the Chapel at Assembly'. Miss Lane's kindly brown eyes twinkled as she graciously accepted the invitation.

Phyl Mullins (Hodges) and her fellow Sixth Formers in their paper grass skirts, 1944

Everyone did war work of some sort. In the early days of the war we made swabs at the Eye Infirmary [now the Hotel Barcelona], which was second only to Moorfields. Hardly vital but it was the 'doing' that mattered. Then we helped at a canteen for soldiers under the watchful eye of members of staff. There, we dished out dreadful watery tea, slices of 'yellow peril' (a widely-given name to Madeira Cake of the time which was a strangely vivid yellow!), and sardine sandwiches. I dread to think how high the bacteria count was in the sopping wet tea towels! Later, I worked at the Allied Services Canteen which was hard work and a long walk home afterwards as there were no buses to Countess Wear on a Sunday. Eventually, I helped at the American camp built on the Golf Course at Countess Wear. Yes, they did try and date me (and my mother!), but in the main they were a lot of homesick, very frightened young men. The prospect ahead was daunting. The highlight of 'my' war was dancing there once to Glen Miller's band.

Fund-raising had its highlights too! To raise money for Tony's parcels, I drilled friends in dance routines which we performed in the school hall and charged Maynardians an entrance fee. I remember well the amused, surprised faces of staff as we hula-hula'd onto the stage in paper grass skirts. The 'Army Air Corps' number was snappy with lots of 'boxes' (a dance step making lots of squares).

Staff changes, as the 'young' ones were called up, were unsettling, as were visits from friends who had joined the Forces. I remember Biddy Coombe, smart in uniform, coming to see us. School seemed almost childish by comparison. We did grow up quickly during those war years. It was inevitable. On the whole, school life deep down was as normal as it could be in the circumstances. We were encouraged to work, play games, and get on with life without making a great production number of it. In later years, I wondered how members of staff coped. They must have had their deep fears for loved ones too. The girls in their charge were a huge responsibility in those unpredictable and uncertain times but they never appeared to be worried. Full marks to them all!

Enjoying a picnic in the School grounds, c1940

Since leaving Maynard, after qualifying as a pharmacist (thank you 'Andy' for all those dreaded Latin lessons!), through my involvement in the Workers' Educational Association, the Literacy Scheme, governor of schools, raising two sons, and now in the University of the 3rd Age, I have appreciated the love of learning and maintaining an enquiring mind that was instilled in us at Maynard. Yes, it was and is a great school. We had an outstanding Head in Miss Ryan and great teaching staff. The Maynardian girls were a great bunch too!

1945–1957

Patricia Williams (Shambrook)

My Traceyville memories are hazy – in Kindergarten and Transition, our afternoon rest on mattresses in the Hall, while looking out through the floor-to-ceiling windows onto the Tennis and Netball courts; the arrival of the Jungle Gym (climbing frame) in the playground – a great event and much enjoyed, and in Form 2 it felt special to be allowed to exit the building by the fire escape which, I seem to remember, had few safety features.

PE in navy blue knickers, 1956

On moving up to main school the setting for the next few years was a building with a warm, imposing frontage, attractive sloping gardens and drive sweeping down to the road. Inside, the feature which most stays in the memory is the wide staircase up to the hall, and the hall itself, with its wall bars, ropes, stage, and windows featuring the poets Chaucer, Spencer, Shakespeare, Bacon and Milton. The hall conjures up memories of PE in navy blue knickers and aertex shirts, daily assemblies, GCE examinations, an after-school country dance club and as the set for the school's participation in BBC Radio's 'Top of the Form' competition.

I have special memories of the Geography room, with its double desks, and the dais where Miss Murray sat. With her use of the rotating blackboards and the occasional 'filmshow', she always made her subject accessible and interesting.

Less pleasing to me was the Cookery room, where one notable failure was my attempt to toss a pancake. Surrounded by neatly tossed pancakes, mine went hurtling across the room, to be scraped off the floor back into the pan.

The corner of the wall outside the Science lab has a particular memory for me. One lunch time, having returned early from 'home dinners', I had gone into the cloakroom (against the rules). On rushing back out, I collided with Miss Gabb and ended up against the wall, with blood pouring from my head. This resulted in stitches in my head, but no reprimand for breaking the rules.

Maynard Team in 1953 recording in the School Hall for 'Top of the Form, the BBC's popular radio quiz show in the 50s and 60s. Team members were Elizabeth Hatch (16), Ann Tribble (14), Hilary Taylor (13), and Gay Addenbrooke (12) (later Head Girl). Sadly, we lost 30–31 to Kidderminster Girls' Grammar School.

As for outside, Athletics on New Grass and Rounders on Leebourne stick in the memory. Round the corner from Waterloo, the outside toilets, was the Fives Court for tennis practice. I enjoyed the opportunity to use the tennis courts during the holidays. Further away, but within walking distance, was the playing field at Heavitree. Hockey was never my thing, and as my house was near the field, I sometimes got lost on the way. No one ever queried my absence, unsurprisingly, I guess!

Looking back, I am thankful for the good educational grounding received at Maynard, and the interests fostered in those formative years.

1947–1954

Margaret Godsland

A Shock

We all sat in the classroom mostly silent, nervous and with the odd, very subdued, whisper: 'Where's the teacher?' We were all from schools, probably mostly state primaries, where French had not been taught, awaiting our first French lesson and no teacher was present!

Suddenly, a door within the classroom (which I discovered many years later to be the entrance to a store cupboard), burst open. A madly gesticulating, expressive figure emerged, showing much facial expression and gabbling incomprehensibly. This was our first introduction to Serge/Miss Sergent, the French teacher, who, of course, was giving us a torrent of French spoken and demonstrated gesturally in the French manner, though we did not know it!

The subject was taught *entirely* in French for the whole of the year, the only English being used to teach international phonetics, so as to show us the sounds that were distinct to the French language!

I still remember Miss Sergeant asking us all what our names were in French, going round the classroom repeating the phrase to each person. Of course, the penny began to drop, when some girls' first names were very similar in both languages. I remember objects in the classroom being taught in a similar way.

Sadly, in the next year, when the two groups of former French and new French learners were amalgamated, my group (1) passed to Claribel/Miss Harding – the teacher automatically translating French into English, if a pupil did not know; rote-learning of long lists of vocabulary; and a juvenile text with farm animals talking!

My first year of French was always very dynamic, lively, challenging and interesting. I later learnt that this way of teaching foreign languages was known as the 'direct' method. It was quite mind-blowing. I don't think I encountered anything as exciting as this in the language field, until I did German with a native Austrian German speaker as an adult.

Vegetarian Ventures

A vegetarian had joined the school! No-one really knew what this was in those days, as it was very unusual. I only took a packed lunch and stayed at school once a week, when I had a lunch-hour music lesson and so had no time to cycle home.

At the table of about eight, some, to us, very strange food was produced: banana bars, Yeastvite sandwiches, Nutella (nutty) bars, Nutella sandwiches, 'artificial' meat, and so on. The vegetarian, who was meant not to eat meat and fish, would exchange her strange food for such delights – for her – of beef-spread sandwiches, various types of fish-paste sandwiches, luncheon meat, spam, or corned beef rolls – or such like. She also enjoyed sweet cakes and sweets and chocolate, which she would not normally have at home. We, in turn, tasted her strange foods. There was a mutual curiosity and a mutual satisfaction with the differing foods tasted on both sides.

I dread to think what her strict vegetarian parents would have thought of all this if they had known!

Summoned to the Presence

Once, when I was in Upper 5, I was summoned to the PRESENCE – in other words, Miss Ryan! This was an extremely rare event, as generally things were dealt with in School Assemblies or by the class teacher. Mostly, summons to see the Head, who in those days was held in some awe, were usually for those very extreme infringements of the school rules, which often led to a girl being at the point of bordering on expulsion.

There was a system of Order Marks and Conduct Marks within the school. The former were awarded for such offences as talking, extremely poor homework or for being a little rude or disobedient. The latter were for really serious offences of a major type and the awarding of, I think, four, led to an expulsion.

I discovered that I had to see Miss Ryan, because I had obtained three Order Marks, all for talking in the corridor – we were meant to walk in complete silence, on the left-hand side of the corridor. Miss Ryan told me that I was an 'absolute disgrace', as she had never before known a 'gal' (she always used this pronunciation) obtain even one order mark in the Upper 5th. She said that she thought that I was the very first girl in the School to have ever done such a disgraceful thing!

Whether this was so or not, I shall never know! However, it had the desired effect – I never had another Order Mark.

Momentous Assemblies

1928, so shortly before Miss Ryan's time, but presumably these were Exeter School boys?!

The Rhino/Miss Ryan was a great one for use of the lengthy, pregnant pause and dramatic emphasis in Assemblies. I am sure she made many important and notable pronouncements but I remember two of a rather different nature!

1. 'It has come to my notice that a Maynard-GAL – has been seen – near the swimming-BATH – in a – RAIN-HAT!!!!!'

The point of this was that such things were not to be used by 'Maynard gals', who were meant to wear black berets (and not their summer panamas or their winter velours) in wet weather!

2. 'It has been REPORTED – to ME – that – a MAYNARD-GAL – has been SEEN – by the CLOCKTOWER – with – a – HELE'S – SCHOOLBOY (scorn personified!)'.

The significance of the Clocktower and Hele's was that this was the state, as opposed to the non-direct grant, Grammar School for boys in the City. Part of the old red building can still be seen on the site of the Exeter College which is near the Clock Tower.

Only Exeter School boys were considered to be good enough for Maynard gals!

An Event in History

History A-level taught in the Sixth Form was of a solid lecture type – almost always continuous dictation for two periods of 70 or 80 minutes. An idea of the quantity of material is demonstrated by the fact that almost 13 thick narrow-lined Science notebooks were full at the end of the course! A pin could be heard dropped in the lessons it was so quiet, as the formidable Ma B/Mrs Bennett was the teacher.

One day in Room 13, there was a silent ripple of smiles and glances, as the odd bit of plaster unexpectedly fell from the ceiling onto the heads of girls sitting in the middle of the room. One or two murmurs drew the attention of Ma B, but she could see nothing amiss.

A little later, a crack appeared in the ceiling, a bit further towards the front of the room and nearer to the teacher. A feeling of unease within the classroom was growing but Ma B could still discern nothing. More little bits of plaster loosened and fell on people's heads and there were one or two more obvious giggles, to the annoyance and consternation of the teacher.

Then things began to happen more swiftly and at a quickening pace …

First, part of a shoe obtruded through the ceiling; then a full foot. Plaster was now descending in showers and, being almost over Ma B's head, she looked up in horror – by now there were two feet hanging down and these were rapidly followed by the descent of a pair of black-nyloned legs. The descent stopped at the point were two black-stockinged feet and a pair of nurse's black, buttoned shoes, suspenders and regulation navy-blue, interlock knickers could be seen. Presumably the bulge of underwear and tunic and possibly spread arms had stopped a further descent!

The girl concerned was a Sixth Former. She had, apparently, entered the out-of-bounds roof space via the small door at the back of the attic Art room and had determined to walk along the joists from one end of the School to the other. She had, not unexpectedly, slipped off the joists onto the plaster between and thus gone through the ceiling above Room 13. She had very nearly achieved her goal – the Library. I think she had thought she could descend through a trap-door in the ceiling at that point.

Rescue involved people working their way along the same route as the unfortunate girl and her being lowered through the ceiling trap-door onto a ladder in the classroom, where we were all seated and watching in amazement – at least the lengthy dictations were disturbed in this one, eventful, lesson!

Upper 5 entertainment, 1952: The Moderns, The Old Girls, The Elizabethans.

Remembering the early Headmistresses

The early 'Maynard' School, the Blue Maids Hospital in Mary Arches Street, was run by the City Council, which employed the Mistress and the Steward who inspected the School regularly and provided funds from the endowment money for food, and new clothing when necessary. The three Minute Books which survive run from 1672 to the 1730s, and give the names of the first two mistresses on record in July 1672 when Mrs Margaret Waters was appointed on the death of 'the late mistress of his House', Mrs Bastarde, whose accounts were ordered to be audited. The role of the mistress in this period was more like that of a matron, who had responsibility also for teaching the girls basic literacy skills, needlework, and, of course, religious instruction. Sometimes, the educational responsibilities of the mistress were not carried out very well, and she had to be reminded of her duties; the reminder duly noted in the Minute Books. We do not know the identities of all the mistresses in this first half of the School's history but the few names we do are as follows:

1672 Mrs Margaret Waters takes charge of school from Mrs Bastarde.

1689 Mrs Margaret Pawle, daughter of Mrs Waters takes over as head of school.

1690 Mrs Udall, daughter of Mrs Pawle, takes over as head of school.

1629 Mrs Udall leaves; Mrs Willmott Martin takes over as head of school.

1707 Mrs Martin dies. Mrs Burrington, a relation, takes over temporarily for two months. Permanent appointment in September of Mrs Mary Gist.

1723 Elizabeth Gist, Mary Gist's daughter, takes over as head.

1731 Mrs Margaret Mayne takes over as head.

1737 Mrs Susannah Morris takes over as head and remains in post until her death in 1782.

Finally, a Jane Dicker is listed in both 1827 and 1831 editions of Besley's Directory for Exeter as 'present mistress of the Blue Maids' School'.

1947–1956

Susan Allison (Burdett)

I first attended the Maynard School in the summer of 1947, having moved from Nottinghamshire. As there was no room for me in Traceyville, the Junior School, I was put into Lower 3 where the other girls were a year older than I was. My sister, two years younger, was in the Junior School.

The main building is more or less as it is today – there were four tennis courts, a boarding house (Tregear), the Junior School (Traceyville) which had a garden, the Headmistress's garden (Miss Ryan's garden in my day, which we were not allowed into), the front drive which only prefects could use and the side steps up from Barnfield Road which the rest of us used, two large areas of grass, one of which was lined with trees which we used to play in. We played Rounders on the smaller area and Hockey on the larger one, also 'horses' in our leisure time (one girl being the horse and the other the rider, using our girdles for reins).

Being younger than the rest of the form and new, I did not fit in very well, was always shy and did badly in work which I didn't always understand. I passed the eleven-plus examination and went on to Upper 3 and Lower 4 before staying down for another year in Lower 4 with a new set of girls. There were some boarders and some private pupils, but if you passed the eleven-plus you then had a free place, as the School was Direct Grant Grammar. Once in a form of girls of my age I did better and was usually top of the class. In fact there was great rivalry between me and Ruth Cockram who was always top of the Parallel form, as to which of us had the higher average mark for end-of-term exams. We were split up into houses: Goldsmiths (the best house – mine, blue), Armourers (green) Merchants (red) and Haberdashers (yellow) and it was important to do well in everything for your House. We had house meetings run by the head of the house and if you had done badly in the current Class List (grades for your work) or, even worse, got Order Marks (bad), or Conduct Marks (terrible) you were in deep trouble. I remember one girl getting caught by Mrs Bennett on the terrace at the front of the School – we always lined up there before Dinner but we weren't supposed to until the bell rang, so when Mrs Bennett issued out with the bell, all fire and brimstone, from the front door, she recalled the last girl racing out of sight round the corner and gave her a Conduct Mark. Most unfair really, but that was discipline *(pour encourager les autres,* etc …). The poor girl couldn't speak when questioned about this in House Meeting – she was overcome! I don't know if Mrs Bennett realised the seriousness of a Conduct Mark, much worse than an Order Mark! Anyway it was all processed at the end of each term and houses were put in order of how well they had done – we played for houses in Netball and Hockey matches as far as I remember. In the winter we sometimes played impromptu Hockey in the lunch hour on the tennis courts because they were icy and it was exciting – I once hit somebody on the mouth and 'killed' one of her front teeth – I've always felt guilty about that.

Miss Ryan was Headmistress during my time at school. She was a good Head and ran the School very much in the old conventional way – the staff had to be very respectful. She had her own room and to be summoned there was worrying, to say the least. As my academic work was good she was always nice to me, but she knew nothing about music which I was very keen on, and couldn't understand anyone wanting to be anything other than an academic university graduate. Going into nursing or music was frowned on if you were good at other things too. Most of the teachers were unmarried, and if they got married they usually left. I had piano lessons in school with Miss Watts and later with Mrs Locke who dyed her grey hair purple and smoked but was very jolly and was a good pianist and teacher. She had her own studio in Exeter and when she fell out with the School we went there for lessons on Saturday mornings. She had a lovely old cottage at Christow, a husband younger than herself and knew Julius Isserlis, pianist (father of Stephen Isserlis, the cellist). We had Miss Forshew for Maths, then Miss Comerford who made me very nervous, Miss Haddow for History and later Mrs Bennett who was a wonderful teacher but slightly alarming at times. We had Miss Lane for English and we had to write essays every week and then she would read them out in class. We had Miss Langhorne for Art. She didn't like you if you couldn't draw and was rather impatient; after an Art exam she would put the pictures up in class and we had to analyse what was good or bad about them. When I first entered the Maynard we used to paint with poster paints (made from powder), first drawing with charcoal and then painting over it. My first picture was sent to a London Children's Exhibition by Miss Langhorne and it was used on the poster advertising the exhibition on the Underground.

Concerts took place occasionally, either given by visiting musicians or by selected school pupils. We also had film shows, very rarely, but red-letter days when they happened. I remember seeing *Lilac Time*, a film about

Schubert, which made me cry, and also *South With Scott* (starring John Mills), with its music by Vaughan Williams. We had some trips (mainly in the Sixth Form I think), one with my History group and Mrs Bennett to Forde Abbey when we were studying medieval monasteries, and one with Miss Anderson to Bradfield School in Reading to watch a Greek play, in Greek, in their open air amphitheatre – a memorable experience. Prize-giving took place once a year, when one received a book for excellence in exams (we had to choose what we wanted beforehand). Greek plays were also performed by school pupils, in English, and sometimes the choir sang for them. We thought they were very well done. Miss Langhorne was very involved in making costumes and Mrs Lloyd in coaching the actors. Upper 5 always did a play or variety entertainment after O-levels were finished in the summer term when they had no lessons so had time to prepare. We did songs, little plays, comedy sketches and dancing for our effort. The whole school would come to the finished article. I used to get permission to go out of school to take part in the Devon Music Festival in Exeter in the spring, either in Elocution classes which quite a lot of us did (also Choral Verse speaking in groups), or for piano classes, either solo or with my sister in duet classes.

Prize Giving 1953 (or Speech Day as it was then called). Dame Janet Vaughan (Principal of Somerville College, Oxford) presenting a prize to Head Girl Marion Sampson with Miss Ryan looking on.

Sport consisted of Gym classes, Hockey, Netball and Cricket (the latter lapsed during the time I was there) and Rounders. To play Hockey or Cricket we had to walk to the hockey field which was about a mile away, so this was usually a full afternoon's activity. We also had to come out of school for Swimming in the summer term, walking to the swimming baths at the end of Denmark Road. I liked Gym, Hockey and Swimming but not Netball. I played in the school hockey teams for many years – matches took all Saturday morning and were quite a commitment. We were not very good and didn't win very often. In the Sixth Form I gave up playing for the School as by then I found homework for A-level plus piano practice (two or three hours a day) was taking all my time. I got taken to task for this (letting down the school, etc., in spite of having done it for years), by the Games Teacher and then by Miss Sargent (French) in front of the whole class, which I have always felt was very unfair (there, I've got that off my chest after all these years!) In the third year in the Sixth I went back to playing in matches for a while, having decided that I had got Grade 8 piano and was not going to take it up as a profession, so didn't need to practise so much.

School rules had to be kept, for example, silence in corridors, being punctual, changing shoes, and so on, but of course they weren't always. The School Song was soon learnt by everybody as we sang it at the end of every term and on Speech Days.

My journey to school was from the village of Whitestone, up and down a lot of hills outside Exeter. There was a bus to within a mile of where we lived and we had free season tickets after we had passed the eleven-plus exam. Getting to an exam was a nightmare in February on icy roads – I was late for it after a hair-raising ride; I'm surprised I passed! Then we had to walk from Exeter Bus Station at the other end which took 20 minutes; as the bus didn't get in until 8.40am we were often late for school, which was very trying for everyone. My father often took us in the car, but as he was bad about getting up in the mornings we were still often late, having rushed down the lanes at high speed which was not conducive to a calm mind at the beginning of the day. We moved into Exeter when I was in the Sixth Form and I then cycled to school, so arrived more punctually.

I got six O-levels and three A-levels at school and went to Bedford College, London University, where I read History, which I really enjoyed.

1951–1961

Ruth Binney (Chanter)

When I started at the Maynard in 1951, in Traceyville, I was one of a small number who travelled in from Tiverton – a group that included my elder sister Lois (Chanter). It made for a long day, especially for the first few years when we cycled to Tiverton station to catch the 'Tivvy Bumper' to Exeter St David's and walked to school from there. Since our parents did not subscribe us to bun tickets we were both agreed that to get one from a friend was a real bonus as with a very early start hunger set in well before lunch time. The only problem was deciding between the delicious choices of cream or Chelsea or iced bun.

Haberdashers' Picnic, 1961

In Traceyville, the youngest pupils would lie down on mattresses in the hall for a rest after lunch, and I remember this in my first year. In the senior school, life was transformed with the opening of the new Dining Centre in 1954, though even then we ate in two sittings. Before that there was a rota in which some people had to bring packed lunches, which I remember eating outside on the terrace on sunny days. Although there were the usual complaints about the lunches, they were not too bad. My favourites were definitely Shepherd's pie and chocolate pudding. I do, however, remember a revolt in which some of us were punished for bringing fretsaw blades into lunch to 'saw' the pastry on the meat pie!

Being mad on sports, I joined in all I could, from games of 'horsey' around Traceyville to endless Netball and Tennis at break times. Although walking to Hockey was a slog, for me it was worth it, and I loved playing in school teams, even if it meant getting home very late. Coming into Exeter on a Saturday to play matches was also enjoyable, as was travelling away to arch rivals such as Exmouth Grammar. Even better were evening Swimming competitions when I either stayed overnight with a friend in Exeter or was given a bed in the boarding house.

The Swimming Gala, held in the pool during the summer term was for me one of the highlights of the sporting calendar, with points scored for your house (I was in Haberdashers). My best achievement was winning the two lengths, but I also loved the 'picking up plates' – the object was to pick up as many from the bottom of the pool without coming up for air. Having practised this endlessly I did once retrieve them all. The other thing that sticks in my mind is the shrill of the spectators which, as you swam, came at you in huge pulses of sound. I remember there were a lot of worries about swimming during the polio epidemics of the 1950s.

Exams were a prominent part of school life, with results being read out in assembly at the end of term for all to hear. Miss Ryan was adamant that seven O-levels were quite enough for anyone, though it meant having to make difficult choices between Geography and History and between a Science and English literature. Ours was the first year in which the top set took Maths a year early – we all passed – which meant that we could add an extra subject the following year. Art was my choice, which I certainly don't regret.

I remember a revolt in which some of us were punished for bringing fretsaw blades into lunch to 'saw' the pastry on the meat pie!

The juniors all joined the seniors for the last assembly of the summer term and it was here that the form lists for the coming year were read out and carriage girdles awarded. Anxiety was high for those of us going up to the senior school, for this was when we were split up into Lower 3 and Lower 3P. I was distraught at being put in the 'P' away from my Tiverton friends, but it doesn't seem so awful in retrospect. On the first day of the new term we were joined by the influx from the eleven-plus which was strange at first, for both them and us. Since the Maynard was then a Direct Grant school, my sister and I were among the fee payers as we lived out of the Exeter area.

One item of 'uniform' that I remember was the shoe bag. These could (I think) be bought, but patterns were also available. They had to be of bright red cotton and were constructed with two pockets, for indoor shoes and gym shoes. They were incredibly complicated to make and even my mother, who was an expert seamstress, had trouble making them. The summer dresses were also tricky and I was lucky that my mother was able to match the shop bought ones almost exactly, with the 'wings' on the sleeves as she did the tunics and striped blouses. Like many families at the time, money was tight, and home-made clothes for all situations the order of the day. As for wearing the uniform, the short tunics made for cold knees in the winter. On rainy days in summer (once Miss Ryan had decreed that it was warm enough for everyone to change into summer dresses), berets were allowed in place of panama hats on rainy days. But whatever the weather it was a school rule that one should never be seen eating in the street in school uniform.

At the beginning of every term, before the first gym lesson, we were all weighed and measured. I was one of the last in the class to reach 5 feet and term after term I was 4ft 11¾, 4ft 11⅞ and so on.

At the end of each term we sang the School Song at the final assembly. That day we were given our reports to take home to our parents. I don't think we would ever have dreamed of steaming them open, but it was tempting!

1950s Hockey team

Speech Day, 1959

Junior production of *'Once Upon a Time'*, 1951

1952

Jennifer Madge (1941–1952), School Secretary 1956–1965 (written for the 1977 school magazine)

The daily pattern of our serene existence was little troubled by events of national importance (though there was guaranteed excitement at the time of a General Election). Wednesday, February 6th, 1952, therefore began as any other day for us. When we set out for School, we were quite unaware of the happenings of that night, leading to the urgent recall of the then Princess Elizabeth from the Treetops Hotel in Kenya. It was not until 12.15 pm that we heard the news of her father's death. Miss Ryan came down to the Prefects' Room to tell us. We were stunned as much as saddened. The future Queen was within 10 years of our own age, and the immense task laid on her shoulders cast a shadow over our own youth.

The following morning at 11am the whole School processed into the hall to listen to the broadcast of the Proclamation of the Accession and, after break that day, to Cathedral Yard for the reading of the official Proclamation there. Movingly in that great crowd, we joined in the singing of the National Anthem. Somehow it had not occurred to us that one day we would sing 'God save the *Queen*'. Eight days later we were led into the hall to hear the broadcast of King George VI's funeral service when, together with the whole nation, we observed a two minutes' silence in memory of a beloved King.

In May of that year the Queen, proclaimed but not yet crowned, attended the Royal Show, which was being held at Newton Abbot. This was a great occasion for the people of Devon and we were fortunate to have a holiday from School to go to the Show if we wished. My diary recalls that I saw the Queen eight times during her visit that day.

So back to 1952, when I was Deputy Head Girl and Business Manager of the Magazine. We were a happy band of prefects, five senior and nine junior, sharing our common task of seeing that the rules, few but well-enforced, were not broken. We met little trouble, though offenders were sternly dealt with and we could, and did, give Order Marks when necessary. We were on duty at the top and bottom of the main staircase, and in the big cloakroom, every morning and afternoon at the beginning and end of School. I can hear our voices now 'DON'T Talk', 'SINGLE File', 'Keep to the left', 'Don't RUN'.

The Prefects' Room, on the bottom corridor next to the main entrance, had just enough room for us, desks and chairs round the walls and one or two easy chairs in the middle. When the days drew in, we had a real fire, and thought we were in the lap of luxury. Every other week Miss Ryan came to coffee (sometimes with the senior prefects, sometimes with all of us) and on one occasion she gave us 20 cups and saucers and a chest to keep them in. I remember those coffee parties – we fetched the coffee and biscuits from the pantry and hid our bun in the desk for afterwards! – and how we used to rack our brains for topics to introduce if the conversation flagged.

1952 was the year when we took A-levels, the first group, I think, to sit for Advanced Level instead of the previous Higher School Certificate. There were about a dozen of us in the Upper Sixth, roughly half Arts and half Science, and one or two third year Sixth as well.

There was a hatch near the door, where the meals appeared brought up from below by a creaking lift.

We were very restricted for accommodation, especially by the spacious standards of today. The hall, the only large space we had, was also the gym, and so reduced in size by parallel bars, ropes, vaulting horse, etc. It was used for prayers, singing lessons as well as gym, public examinations, lunch-hour activities on wet days and as a dining room for the cold dinner girls. I should explain that, because of the limited kitchen facilities, hot dinners could be served for only half the School each day, and so on alternating days we had to bring sandwiches. The dining room was on the top corridor, with a fire escape down to the Fives Court. There was a hatch near the door, where the meals appeared brought up from below by a creaking lift. Singing lessons were held in the dining room, too, and frequently in the afternoons the smell of cabbage lingered.

Beyond the kitchen was the Milk Bar, where we collected our 'Buns and Milk' at break. Near the Milk Bar was the pantry, where Miss Leaman was to be found. She it was who stoked up our fire in the Prefects' Room and, in all manner of ways, gamely contributed to the welfare of staff and girls alike. Every day, a little before

12.50pm, she was to be observed checking her trays of dishes and cutlery ready for laying up lunch in the Staff Room when the bell went. And here I must mention Bridle, who ruled over the 'stoke hole', and us, with equal authority. Behind his somewhat forbidding look, lest we dare to trespass, he was kindness itself. I believe he was always glad to see us back on the first day of term.

Uniform regulations were strict and the wearing of a hat, winter or summer, was a 'must'; in wet weather, and it certainly saved the hat, a beret was permissible. From time to time one period of lessons was given over to an inspection by the Form Mistress when coat, hat, shoe bag, etc., had to be laid before her. This ensured not only that our clothing conformed to the required standards, but that everything was clearly labelled. Winter uniform was worn well into the summer term until the word was given (one morning at Prayers) that we could change into summer dresses. It was an unwritten rule and we had sympathy for the poor unsuspecting new girl who understandably appeared in a summer dress on the first day of the summer term. But it was just not done.

In the Sixth Form we could, if we wished, wear a navy (regulation) skirt instead of a tunic. The skirt much improved our adolescent figures and with black lisle stockings (silk ones were expensive and, in any case, hard to come by) and sensible shoes, we looked quite smart. As prefects, we were privileged to exchange our well-worn navy velours and yellowing panamas for a navy tricorne, old stock purchased from the WRNS. This was before the days of the summer boater, so however hot it was, we still wore our tricornes.

Our out-of-school activities were not many or varied, mainly I suppose because of the size of the Sixth Form. Apart from Games and Music (the Choir and Orchestra were popular and flourishing), I recall only the Scientific Society and the Literary and Debating Society, when we sometimes shared meetings with Exeter School. There was also the Post-War Society, commonly known just as 'Post-war' or 'PWS'. We had a weekly meeting in school time for a talk on the topic for the term – for example, 'Local Government', 'Education', and 'The Press and Communications'. At the end of term we had a Conference Day with the other schools who took part, a joint service, sometimes in the Cathedral, then a lecture on the termly topic, group discussions over a picnic lunch and a Brains Trust in the afternoon. The subject most regularly chosen by the committee of the schools who participated with us was 'Marriage and Family Life' (I think it was as close as we ever discreetly came to anything approaching Sex Education!).

July 16th, 1952, dawned bright and clear for the Sixth Form Picnic, which was the Ascot event of the school calendar. On this one day in the year we were allowed to come to School in 'mufti'. It was a great occasion with much heart-searching among us as to what we would wear. No junior who sat in the hall will forget the sight of the prefects as they paraded on the platform on Picnic Day (in outfits often totally unsuitable for a picnic, of course).

The other social highlight of the school year was the Sixth Form Dance at the end of the Christmas Term. Carefully chaperoned by the Sixth Form staff, we danced in the gaily decorated hall to the music of a well-respected local band, and then made our way to the dining room for supper. We returned (woe betide those who didn't!) for more dancing until 10.30 or 11pm.

Sixth Form Picnic at Belstone, c1952. Note cigarette in the background!

One more memory of summer 1952 – in May there was a large gathering for a rather special Old Girls' Reunion. An 'At Home' on the Saturday afternoon with skipping and a gym display on New Grass and country dancing at Leebourne, was followed by tea and then a dinner in the evening. On the Sunday morning the senior prefects acted as ushers for a service in the hall at 11am when a new stained-glass window which is there today (and was then, presumably, a replacement for war-damage) was unveiled by The Bishop.

Some of my Old Girl contemporaries now have daughters of their own in School, who chuckle when the photograph albums are produced. Time marches on but memories remain and pride that we too, had our place in the continuing achievements of the Maynard.

1958–1962

Jean Hall, Head of English 1958–1987

I have concentrated on the years 1958–62 as the School was still much as it had been for years since the end of the Second World War. The staff had mostly been there for years and changes of staff were rare. In 1960 there was an unusually large entry of new staff and the retirement of Miss Ryan marked the end of an era.

Life under Miss Ryan

I came to the Maynard in 1958 as Head of English, succeeding Miss Lane who had been on the staff since well before the Second World War (30+ years!). I was interviewed by Miss Ryan, who was very friendly and approachable and talked mostly about schools she and I had connections with, before handing me over to Miss Evans, who showed me round the buildings and took me back for tea at her rooms in Lower Summerlands. Here she set about persuading me that I should like the school. I was impressed by the stability and relaxed atmosphere it had, and the welcome I had received by the staff I had met. Miss Lane was ill at the time, and the work was explained to me by Miss Claborough, who was to be my full-time colleague in the English department. We shared the same views and standards and she was to become an invaluable help and good friend. Among other things I was told that the School was celebrating its 300th anniversary, and that they had had a special service in the Cathedral when the staff (unusually) wore hats!

On starting in September, I found a calm orderly school, all wearing school uniform, including hats. The prefects were distinguished by Wren officer-style hats in winter and straw boaters in summer. Pupils had most lessons in their form room, specialised rooms being limited to Art, Domestic Science and the Sciences. New buildings erected fairly recently were the Biology lab, the dining room and the gym. Leebourne, once the site of a bombed house, was the area for break. Games were played on the four tennis courts and on part of the fields where the Royal Devon & Exeter Hospital now stands.

'Britannia' in Dryden's *King Arthur*, 1958

There were few interruptions to normal lessons, except towards the end of the summer term and for rehearsal of the school play in the autumn. This was produced by Mrs Lloyd, who taught Speech and Drama, and was performed at St Luke's Theatre. I was pressed into painting scenery for Dryden's *King Arthur* the highlight of which was the singing of *Fairest Isle* by Britannia, perched on a cloud above waves which I had helped to paint. The English department's contribution to Drama at this time was confined to activity in the form room, with desks pushed back, and occasionally trips into the hall, when it was free, to use the stage. We had a large stock of sets of text books, which had to be distributed, recorded and collected at the beginning and end of each school year. For English we took charge of the literature section so that we could change the texts each term or more frequently.

The Sixth Form was not large. Mrs Bennett was in charge and set high standards. There were only two for A-level English in the Upper Sixth in 1958, but over the years numbers greatly expanded, so that we were able to have two sets in each of Upper and Lower Sixth. I introduced an essay class for all Sixth Formers to keep up a good standard of writing and general comprehension. General Studies were there already in the Post War Society, a joint effort with Exeter School bringing in outside speakers on a variety of topical subjects. The Sixth Form picnic was an enjoyable event at the end of the summer term, when the girls (not in uniform!) had a trip to Dartmoor, Stratford or other chosen venue. New members of staff were always invited and Miss Ryan and Sixth Form staff also took part. I remember Miss Ryan sitting out at Belstone, while the prefects dipped in the river and some of us walked up to the Tor.

Most of the senior staff had been at the School for many years and had stories to tell about fire-watching and the bombing during the war. They were very hospitable and a number entertained me during my first term or two to make me feel at home.

The staff at that time were almost all unmarried. As a result the younger members tended to do things together at weekends. There were excursions to Bude for surfing in the summer and we went walking or to the

Miss Lane with the Upper Fifth, c1933

Miss Lane cutting the cake at her retirement party in 1958. Miss Ryan is in the centre

theatre with friends on the staff. Staff mostly stayed to school dinner, which was eaten at a high table with the girls in the dining room. Later, when the Tregear boarding house was given up, staff had a dining room there. After lunch, oddly, there was no tea or coffee in the staff room. The Science staff were envied as they 'brewed up' in a lab. Nobody had lessons in the dinner hour. Some girls went home, and after lunch staff either walked up to town or helped Miss Anderson with *The Times* crossword. Life was quite leisurely and we had an open fire in the staff room in winter, which was much missed when it eventually disappeared.

Miss Ryan ran the School on very traditional lines. She was quite an impressive figure, but very concerned for the welfare of staff and girls. She was respected and she respected her staff. She appointed people she felt would do the work and left them to carry on without interference. She remembered staff birthdays and took all the staff out to dinner at Dartington.

The Library

In 1958 the library was run by Miss Anderson, Head of Classics. It consisted of the rebuilt traditional library with its bookcases and matching wooden tables and chairs. The catalogue system was the unusual Cheltenham one and borrowings were recorded in a large leather-bound book.

Lower Sixth in the Library, 1949

When Miss Anderson retired, I was asked to take over the library in lieu of being a form mistress. After a while, having trained a team of Sixth Form librarians, I introduced a card system for recording borrowing and late-returned books, including fines, which were used to buy new books in addition to the annual allocation. With the help of one of the many excellent head-librarians from the Sixth Form I was able to reintroduce the Dewey system of cataloguing, as was used in most public libraries.

As school building expanded, the library was able to use the large adjacent form room. This was to be called the General Library while the older library was to be the more specialised one for Sixth Form use. We tried to make the new room as attractive as possible and to put in it all the books of general interest – and attractive appearance. I was always reluctant to turn out any books just because they were not of general interest, as it seemed to me that a good library should provide as wide a coverage as possible. You never know what someone is going to want to find out!

A New Home for the Sixth Form

Margaret Ross, an Upper Sixth-former, writing in late-1970

During the summer holidays. the same question must have crossed the mind of every Maynard Sixth Former at least once – would the block be ready for occupation on the first day of term? The answer, true to the British tradition of compromise, was yes and no: after assembly on the first morning, we were able to move ourselves and our books into the two form rooms on the first floor, hot on the heels of the retreating workmen. What we found there was a pair of light, airy, cheerful classrooms, equipped with practical, adaptable, formica-topped tables and bright chairs, and linked by a block of four inter-connecting studies for the four members of staff into whose care we have been entrusted – Miss Westall, Miss Wickenden, Miss Gabb and Miss James.

Sixth Formers enjoying their new Common Room in the 1970s.

After two weeks of frustrating glimpses of workmen sitting having their tea-break in *our* common room, and seeing interesting-looking kitchen equipment being installed, we were finally able to relax in the comfort of our mustard and olive-green chairs in the common room on Monday, 28th September, and there, reflected upon our unbelievable good fortune in having such luxurious facilities at our disposal. Even now, after using the block for some weeks, one sometimes has the feeling that it is all simply too good to be true, that one grey Monday morning we shall come out of our dream and find the block gone, the old lawn back in its place, and ourselves returned to the cramped conditions of Rooms 5 and 12.

The building's pleasing exterior is surpassed by the masterpiece of planning inside. Our every need has been foreseen and provided for in the most astonishing way: not only the big things, like the superbly equipped coffee bar and kitchen, but smaller, thoughtful additions like lockers, specially made big enough to take our files in our form rooms; permanent coat hangers on racks instead of rows of hooks, and elegant modern units with sunken washbasins in the cloakroom; a strip light over the notice board, and a carpeted, cosy corner in the common room … and so on. We thought we had succeeded in catching the planners out over one matter in the common room: sitting with our mugs of coffee arranged around our feet, we said to ourselves, 'What we really need are some coffee tables'. Imagine our amazement, when the next morning, as if by magic, half a dozen perfect coffee tables were found distributed around the room!

I have been using the term 'the planners' rather loosely throughout; as most people must realise, the mastermind behind all the planning was Miss Bradley, and it is to her that we offer our sincere thanks for making what has for so long been a dream for her, into such a magnificent reality for us.

Official Opening of Ryan House

Heather Griffith, Lower Sixth, writing in 1971

A Tribute to Miss Ryan, Headmistress 1935–62

As a tribute to Miss Elsie May Ryan it was decided to name the new Sixth Form Block and to re-landscape the Headmistress's garden in her memory. During her 27 years as headmistress, Miss Ryan was responsible for the high standard achieved in all fields of school life, but is most remembered by those who knew her for great personality and deep involvement with young people, and it was Miss Ryan who was responsible for the increase of the Sixth Form from 20 to 70 girls during her term of office.

The ceremony to open Ryan House took place on the evening of 2nd July. The service, which was led by the Bishop of Crediton, was held in the gymnasium to accommodate governors, parents, friends, staff and both past and present girls of the School. We were pleased to welcome the brother and family of the late Miss Ryan. Margaret Ross, representing present Maynardians, read a lesson and Alison Beale sang the anthem, 'God be in my head'. After prayers and hymns the guests of honour went to the main door of the new building where a plaque to the memory of Miss Ryan was unveiled. The Bishop spoke a few words of dedication relayed by loud speaker to the congregation in the gymnasium. After the service guests were shown round the Sixth Form Block and other parts of the School where various exhibitions were staged.

Although Ryan House was officially opened only last July, the Sixth Form have been in residence for a year. The common room and coffee bar are much appreciated and several committees are responsible for the smooth running of a changed Sixth Form.

Our debt to Miss Ryan can never be paid, but present and future girls will always be grateful for all she did for the School. Ryan House and the Rose Garden are a small tribute to one to whom we owe so much.

Miss Ryan outside Exeter Cathedral after the Tercentenary Thanksgiving Service in 1958

Remembering Miss Ryan

Gay Waddams (Whitfield), Teacher of PE 1946–49

I was appointed to the staff in September 1946. Miss Ryan interviewed me in London and as it was a late appointment, offered to put me up until I found suitable accommodation.

I lived in the Close with her for six months, and we got on very well. On Sunday mornings we would go off in her open car to Sidmouth, Budleigh or Dawlish Warren, Miss Ryan driving with a cigarette in her mouth, the ash blown off as we speeded through the countryside, and I often got an eyeful of her ash!

That winter of 1946/47 my sister came and stayed. There was deep snow everywhere and she and I climbed onto the roof and cleared four inches of snow! The very thought gives me vertigo!

After leaving the Maynard in 1949 I taught in Portugal where I met and married Don. Miss Ryan spent a jolly holiday with us, albeit losing her passport on arrival which was found in a Hotel in Estoril the day before she left.

We took her to some very lively parties including a wedding. She used to visit us in South Brent and we remained friends for the rest of her life.

1964–1977

Anna Bruce-Jones (Skinner)

Oh, how I loved every moment of my 13 years at the Maynard (well, nearly every moment: finding excuses for not having done homework took some initiative, plus I wasn't too keen on the yearly exams). From my first day I felt as though I had come home, so much so that I spent my last day in tears (and in school uniform, surprisingly, despite being at the end of two years of sixth-form mufti-dom). So when my daughter, Anastasia, won her place at the old alma mater I was thrilled; memories came flooding back. I duly enthused her with tales of:

- Pre-starting letters informing us that each child had to be able to tie her own bow at the back of her art overall (even at the tender age of five) and use the phrase 'Please may I be excused?' when needing the lavatory.
- Post-lunch resting on mats rolled up at the back of Junior School hall (mine was a rather chic faux leopard-skin, I seem to remember).
- Bun and Dinner Tickets (and learning to take turns over who got the jam doughnuts and who was left with the iced buns – 'boring!').
- Daily assemblies singing traditional hymns (very handy at weddings and baptisms – and less happy occasions – when one can look down smugly at those who are unfamiliar with the *Songs of Praise* regulars, whilst one is hardly glancing down at the words).
- Eagerly awaiting the announcement of Carriage Girdle – and, later, Carriage Badge – ('to be added to sundries account') winners at end-of-term assemblies and then singing the school song (favourite line: 'play not for self, but for the side', sung with great gusto) 'Xeroxed' in purple ink, the smell of which made us not a little high, I suspect (or was it just end-of-term high spirits?).
- Indoor and outdoor shoes of strictly specified genus and classification (wasn't one of the pairs Norvik something-or-other? How can I remember that 40 years on, but not where I've parked my car this morning?).
- Running around acres and acres (so it seemed) of Leebourne in the summer or, in winter, climbing around the gigantic oil tank or hanging upside down on the bars, head just two to three feet above the concrete surface of the play area.

Anastasia trying on her Mum's Maynard uniform

So are all these traditions still alive and well at the modern Maynard?

I really should have known that things had changed when the first notification of Anastasia's success in the entrance examinations came from a charming and enthusiastic call from Dr West herself. In person. Yes, really. She even rang from her own home at 8.30 in the evening. Just stop and think. Can you really imagine the wonderful, yet correctly upright, Miss Bradley doing that? Not that we – in common with many people then – had a phone at home in 1964, but that was just not the way things were done in The Old Days. So when I ask Anastasia about what bun she had at lunch time and whether she was a Good Rester, she looks at me with a quizzical (yet sympathetic) look and tells me that things have changed from the 60s and 70s.

Although I might yearn for past times, when I see Mr Smerdon sitting on the floor reading – nay, performing – to an enthralled group of 7- to 10-year-olds, I just cannot imagine dear Miss Sparks crawling on the parquet of the Junior School hall with her tweeds and brogues, and I feel a twinge of envy for the current Maynardians.

The Traceyville Fire, 1972

Miss Bradley's account, as published in 1973

I had spent Saturday, 23rd September 1972, at a conference in London. Over lunch the conversation had at one stage turned to how, for the head of a school, the next knock at the door or the next telephone call can be the beginning of the next crisis. But for me that night it was neither; it was a tap on the shoulder that woke me from a deep sleep at 11.45pm and a voice calmly informed me that the police had just telephoned to say that there was a bad fire in 'Tregear, the Junior School'. The message added that I was not to be frightened but to come at once! Inevitably I felt that I was experiencing a nightmare, but by the time I had donned some old clothes and my wellington boots I considered that I was sufficiently awake to get out my car and drive to school to see if this was real. On the way the contradiction of Tregear and the Junior School nagged at me, the loss of which, I wondered anxiously, would present the greater problems. When I reached the end of Spicer Road East this matter was settled; Tregear stood solid and unconcerned ahead of me, whilst the road in front was lined with hose-pipes running to the right and no traffic was being allowed in that direction.

Firefighting outside of building
(Photo courtesy: Exeter Express & Echo)

I parked the car by the Dining Centre and immediately a young policeman arrived to escort me to Traceyville. His cheerful, 'It's burning merrily, miss,' heightened my apprehension and was hardly necessary, for by now I could hear the crackle of the fire and the crash of falling timbers and slates. As we rounded the corner by the Biology Laboratory I could see that the old original house of Traceyville was engulfed in smoke and flames. I was quickly introduced to the Chief Fire Officer in an oddly formal way in the circumstances. Once I had reassured him that there should have been no one in the building and told him where to contact the caretaker, Mr Harris, he was off to continue his command of operations, which he conducted with such skill that he and his men managed to confine the fire to the old part of the building, leaving the wings that had been added only to suffer smoke damage.

I was left standing rather forlornly, outwardly uninvolved in all the activity as firemen hurried about their duties with the confidence born of discipline and strict training. The young policeman appeared at the top of the fire escape and beckoned me up to have a look. I joined him and we made our way along the smoke-filled, blackened top corridor from which the flames had been beaten back in the nick of time. At the end where the wing joined the old building two firemen stood directing jets of water down into the inferno below. Upper 1's door had been burnt away, and by the light of the fire I could see their paintings stirring on the further wall.

It was no place to stay long and I was glad to get outside again and even more glad to see that Mr Harris had arrived, someone at last to talk to. Almost immediately came a further welcome relief when we were allowed to go into the cloakroom to salvage shoe bags. It was good to have something useful to do, but this task was soon completed and once again I found myself watching dejectedly, this time sitting on the low wall by the tennis court.

It was now nearly 2am and it was obvious that I could be of no further help. It seemed sensible for me to get some sleep, or at least some rest, in readiness for the time when it would be my turn to go into action. When I got home I realised that my clothes smelt horribly of smoke; it was a smell with which we became all too familiar in the weeks to come and which lingered with us for a long time. Before I went back to bed I wrote out my plan of action for the morning, which had been forming in my mind during the last couple of hours and then, unexpectedly, I did manage to get a few hours' sleep.

Fireman outside Upper 1 form room
(Photo courtesy: Exeter Express & Echo)

When I returned to Traceyville later that morning with Miss Sparks [Head of Junior School at the time], the scene was depressing in the extreme and no longer was there the purposeful bustle of the firemen to buoy us along. Thankfully we saw that Mr Norris, the School's architect, and representatives from Woodman's, the builders, had already arrived and these people were the first of the many, many friends of the School who came to our aid in this emergency. The rapidity with which salvage operations were conducted, smoke-damaged rooms were re-decorated and their contents cleaned still amazes me, and no praise is too high for the architect, the builders, the Junior School Staff and Mrs Furlong, so recently appointed domestic bursar, and her cleaners, that they managed to get the Junior School fully operational again a week later.

The next 12 months were to be a very great strain on Miss Sparks and her colleagues. The children quickly adapted themselves to the new situation, some aspects of which they found great fun. Form 2 revelled in their unexpectedly early promotion to being full members of the Main School; they were the only people who were glad that the Junior School was not rebuilt in time for them to return to their own form room; they would have viewed such demotion with disgust!

Investigations as to how the fire had started dragged on, and we got quite a guilt complex about what we had kept under the stairs where the fire had been proved to have started. Consciences were greatly relieved when we learnt that it had been arson and that the fire-raisers had been apprehended when attempting to start their fifth fire in their third school. In the new building there is no cupboard under the stairs!

The Governors have ensured that this ill-wind should be turned to good use, and the new building is a great improvement; the Kindergarten and Upper 1 rooms are much more spacious and light. As I write this just over a year later, it is a pleasure to record that the Junior School community is complete again and that the staff, who battled so cheerfully with the inconveniences and the noise of the re-building, are now enjoying their new surroundings to the full.

The morning after the fire
(Photo courtesy: Western Morning News)

Becoming Fully Independent

Miss Bradley's statement, published in 1975

1975 has been a momentous year in the School's history. It is matched only by the year 1922. In that year the School offered to forego its independence on the financial side and accept Direct Grant status in order that its doors could be opened to children from a much wider social background. In the intervening 53 years we have been able to play a major part in providing a rich educational environment for girls in Exeter and the surrounding area who had the kind of ability to benefit from a strongly academically-biased curriculum.

This year the Government has presented the School, along with all the other Direct Grant Schools in the country, with an ultimatum either to enter the state system and accept whatever role the LEA [Local Education Authority] offers, or to revert to full independence. The first alternative would mean abandoning our specialised curriculum and losing our Sixth Form and probably our identity; the second would almost certainly mean closing our doors to academically-able children from less-affluent homes. After lengthy consultations and much deliberation and heart-searching, it was decided to revert to full independence.

It was heartening at the time of making this difficult decision last July to learn the strength of the local support for the School. The signatures on our petition eventually numbered over 14,900, and we could have collected more given more time. A small group went to the lobby at the Houses of Parliament on June 24th. We were with some 5,000 others, and the normal organisation for a lobby at Westminster was quite unable to cope with such a large number. How good it was to see a vast concourse of orderly, determined people quietly demanding that Direct Grant Schools should be IN, rather than the more usual noisy demonstrators mindlessly yelling OUT. These activities and the many, many letters written to MPs have, alas, had no effect on the Government's decision, but they have established the widespread support which these schools enjoy and which cuts across political party boundaries.

Miss Bradley planting a tree outside the Dining Centre (where Pring is now), to mark the Queen's Silver Jubilee, October 1977

Life in Upper 3P 1975 and Sixth Form 1982–1984

Catherine Hill (Savage) 1975–1984

The large brass handbell was already being rung at the bottom of the hall stairs as the Bovey bus arrived. Just time to throw coats onto pegs, which were already festooned with regulation red cotton shoe bags and blue wrap-over science overalls. We rushed upstairs to Room 14 to find registration finishing, so we joined the silent procession back along the tiled corridor to the hall for assembly. Packed in like sardines, if we wanted to sit cross-legged on the floor for the reading and prayers, the trick was to start dipping downwards before the end of the hymn: mistime it and there was only pins-and-needles-inducing kneeling space left.

Many of our lessons were in our form room, where we sat perched on the fixed benches of generations-old desks. The teacher was also perched, her equally venerable desk and stool raised on a dais in the corner. The large roll-round blackboard was used heavily. There were no photocopiers so worksheets were relatively rare; produced on a Banda machine, they were purple or turquoise with a distinctive smell. We were expert at taking down dictated notes. For French, we moved down the corridor to Room 15 to watch film strips of the Bertillon family's adventures – one of us had the job of winding the projector on from picture to picture. Geography was in Room 12, the huge double wooden desks there having fold-over map tables so that an OS map could be laid out flat. Double Science often meant practicals, such as carrying out flame tests and making a microbalance.

Lunchtime, and given that the rota was strictly ordered by age, the endless wait was usually spent roller skating on Bottom Court. The canvas purse belts which we all wore came into their own as tow bars, allowing us to link up as a long train. In the autumn, we might instead be found under the large horse chestnut tree by the gym, waiting for Sixth Formers, who were allowed to cross the Rose Garden and so might pick up out-of-bounds conkers for us. At last able to queue for lunch, we gave our dinner tickets in under the watchful eye of the Upper 5s on duty. Mrs Furlong's food was excellent: highlights were the hunks of freshly-baked granary bread each day, lasagne (in an age where pasta at home was limited to tinned spaghetti), and fruit salad with homemade shortbread. Afterwards, many of us would visit the tuck shop. Crisps, one flavour only but a different one each day, were 5p; Daleks, ice lollies made from chocolate and mint ice cream – the height of sophistication – were 6p.

Miss Bradley (left), laying the new sports hall's foundation stone, with Miss Murdin (right) and other members of staff looking on, 1984.

Afternoons might mean Hockey, with a chilly walk up to the pitches at Exeter School. Permission to wear tracksuit trousers instead of flimsy games skirts was a battle which was only won later. If it was raining hard enough, we did country dancing in the hall instead. Or we might be in the needlework room on the ground floor of Tregear, all making skirts to an identical pattern. The sewing machines were hand operated, so there were no shortcuts when neatening raw edges or making buttonholes. And then the last bell of the day sent us running down the path to the main entrance for the slow bus ride home.

Fast forward five years, to the Sixth Form … and our turn to retrieve the Rose Garden conkers for the youngsters. A-levels and university entrance were the priorities and studying kept us busy. Miss Hamilton's Maths lessons covered a lot of ground quickly, whilst still being great fun. As we worked through exercises, she had the uncanny knack of sensing a mistake, even from the other side of the room. Chemistry was in the General Science lab, which was little changed from its original 1882 state. It was easy to let imaginations drift back to the pioneering women scientists who had been taught there. But there was little time for day dreaming: Mrs Wigg's sharp eye for detail and outstanding mental arithmetic skills meant that we needed our wits about us. Mr Swift's approach in Physics was rather more relaxed, and we often digressed into the then topical issues of nuclear power and the Advanced Passenger Train. As lab space was limited, for most lessons we were shoehorned into the Science prep room, which we shared with the School's only computer, a Research Machines 380Z.

As much a part of the Sixth Form, though, was our non-academic life. Lunchtimes were hectic, perhaps filled with Netball practice, a dash to the Magdalen Road bakery to buy a snack and then a choir rehearsal, or organising activities for 20 or so junior pupils at Maths Club or Junior Christian Union. General Studies offered the chance of a game of Hockey or the freedom of the Art room for the afternoon.

And so to A-level exams. As we lined up nervously outside the gym, clutching the cushions which we took with us to lessen the discomfort of three hours on saggy canvas chairs, it was hard to believe how rapidly our time at school had disappeared.

Group of Lower 5 pupils, c1982

Lunchtime, and given that the rota was strictly ordered by age, the endless wait was usually spent roller skating on Bottom Court. The canvas purse belts which we all wore came into their own as tow bars, allowing us to link up as a long train.

Veronica Clarke (Westall) 1966–1988, English teacher; later Head of Sixth Form

When I started at the Maynard there was no video and certainly no computers; I remember when the School got a video (Betamax – wrong system!), it did make a difference to teaching English, particularly Shakespeare.

Those were the days of O-levels and A-levels, no AS-levels, GCSE's or coursework. They weren't necessarily better or worse days – just different.

What was the same was the friendly atmosphere and the stimulating company of colleagues and students alike.

1997–2007

Karla-Luise Herpoldt

(currently reading Physics at Lady Margaret Hall, Oxford University)

Sitting in triple French on a Wednesday afternoon, the day seemed like it would never end; a friend and I created a game where the person who lost was the person who looked at the clock first. Neither of us was ever very good, I don't think we ever made it past a minute or two. Yet suddenly my days at the Maynard are over and the last 10 years seem to have flown by.

I was at the Maynard from 1997 to 2007 and whilst there, witnessed the School transform to meet the new millennium. When I joined the School Miss Murdin was headmistress. The one lasting memory I have of her (not that in Upper 1 you saw much of her), was one mufti day where I met her, walking through the Traceyville playground, dressed in full uniform; her kilt rolled up high, shirt un-tucked under her jumper and her hair scraped into a pony tail that sat balanced precariously on the crown of her head. She stopped to talk with us and as she left I remember being in awe at this woman who was in charge of the school, but who still had the time to laugh with her very youngest girls and dress up to cause a smile.

A year later she retired and we saw the arrival of Dr West who brought with her new ideas and energy (though those who remembered Miss Murdin always mourned the loss of the 10 o'clock start on the first day of term!). Thankfully, Dr West also got rid of the triple lessons in the afternoon, which made Wednesday afternoons seem to go much faster!

Karla-Luise (left) and her Upper Sixth Maths group with their Pi cake, 2007.

The new millennium meant that the School had to change to keep up. In the Junior School, ICT lessons still posed somewhat of a problem. If the whole class tried to use the same program at the same time, or view the same website, the School network would crash and the lesson would be wasted, not always a bad thing aged seven! By the time we reached Sixth Form, the thought of the whole year not being able to browse Facebook at the same time seemed ridiculous – it's funny how things can change so fast!

In Sixth Form we were lucky enough to have the shiny (and still relatively new) Sixth Form Centre all to ourselves. I can remember it being built – sat in the Chemistry labs in the middle of the summer term, we had the perfect view over the building work. Admittedly on the hot days, Dr Allen found it difficult to keep our attention, after all, to a 15-year-old girl, which is more exciting, chemical reactions or topless builders?!

Dr Allen was just one of the many amazing teachers I had over the years. Each one was unique and totally different and each has left me with countless happy memories. Each taught me something, whether it was academic or not, whether they meant to teach that particular lesson or not.

Some memories are more vivid than others; being made to run up Paris Street en masse because we were late for a sports class was hugely embarrassing at the time, 20 young Maynardians racing past little old ladies with their shopping bags, just off the bus, was quite a sight to behold! Residential trips to adventure centres where we outwitted the instructors and I fell into the mud off my mountain bike countless times, hiding under our desks when a teacher left the room and Science classes where explosions were common!

I was told by my grandmother that I should relish my days at school because they would be the best times of my life. At the time I didn't take her too seriously. Now that they're over, and 10 years have disappeared, I understand exactly what she meant. The experiences of the Maynard will never leave me, memories that will stay with me forever and I know that in years to come when we, the class of '07, gather together again, we will indeed 'set the halls a-ringing, with laughter bred of memories'.

How we celebrated 350 years

The Maynard School marked its 350th year with a rich and varied programme of events during 2008, some just within the immediate School community; others for the wider community: pupils, parents, former pupils and friends. Here is just a flavour of an unforgettable year for all involved.

350 Human Logo

Shortly before February half-term, the whole School stopped lessons briefly one morning to gather outside Tregear and replicate the now-familiar 350th logo. This specially-designed logo was based on the three red hands from Sir John Maynard's original coat of arms. Aerial photographs were taken of the pupils and staff wearing appropriate colours and holding high their letters proclaiming 'The Maynard School – 350 years – 1658–2008', as they formed the logo on the ground. The celebratory event was made even more memorable by the presence of Ms Bee Hughes, the new Headmistress taking up her post in January 2009. Afterwards everyone went to the Main Hall where Ms Hughes and Headmistress Dr Daphne West cut a huge celebration cake for the whole School.

'A Celebration of Art' Exhibition

Over a long sunny weekend, 11th–13th April, the celebrations stepped up with a major exhibition and sale of contemporary art. The School and its grounds provided a wonderful setting for a diverse range of exhibits, including paintings, sculpture, photographs, ceramics, jewellery and furniture, from 157 local, national and international artists, including a rare John Piper ink and gouache work which was snapped up in the first hour. The exhibition was opened on the Friday night by Alan Cotton, one of Britain's most distinguished landscape painters. In conjunction with the exhibition, the School also held an art competition for Sixth Form art students throughout Devon. This was judged by Alan Cotton and all the students' artwork was included in the exhibition. Well over 1,000 people visited the exhibition, with art enthusiasts travelling from as far afield as Oxford, and sales over the weekend totalled in excess of an astonishing £59,000, which raised nearly £14,000 for the School. The profits from this event will be used to fund a means-tested bursary for a new Maynard Sixth Form Art Scholarship.

Opening of Murdin Link

On 3rd May, Felicity Murdin (Headmistress 1980–99), opened the exciting new building which bears her name. The Murdin Link replaced the prefabricated, 'temporary' Hauser building which was erected after the bomb damage in 1942. It had been used, most recently, as Lower 3 form rooms and for senior Geography teaching. The new building is a two-story, five-classroom block which also provides improved staff offices and enhanced disabled access to the School site. The Murdin Link also connects with the main building via the library corridor and will ultimately link with the Junior Department when it is refurbished in 2009/10. The Link has provided a light, airy, spacious addition to the School's facilities and is a triumph, not only for the architects who came up with the inspired design, but also for the builders who rose magnificently to the challenge of constructing it in such a restricted space.

School Picnic

Claudia Beresford (Lower 1)

On Tuesday [6th May], we had our school picnic. We got into our houses (Goldsmiths, Haberdashers, Merchants and Armourers). We had hot dogs and lots of yummy food. Then it was time for the Sixth Form tug-of-war. It must have been very tricky but it was very entertaining. Then some of us had face paint, but only if we wanted to. Then we went into Bradley Hall for some Country Dancing with Mrs Wood and Miss Millar. And then the best bit — the races! It was so much fun; I loved it. First the egg and spoon race, then the sack race and the sprint and then the potato race. The next game was worm charming where you had to pick up the worms with your hands. Merchants got 16, Armourers 29, Haberdashers 20 and Goldsmiths 48. Then we had a game of musical statues. Soon we came to the end of the day but we were all happy because we knew that we had had the best day.

Sarah Tresidder (Lower Sixth; Head Girl 2008–09)

At lunchtime, the whole school gathered on Leebourne for what proved to be a very entertaining picnic and afternoon's activities. The Upper Sixth had arranged through several meetings within their houses for specific foods to be brought in by year groups (for example, the juniors brought cakes), and a contribution by the kitchen of delicious hot dogs and juice was also made. It had been decided that it would be nice and probably more organised if we ate within our houses too, so everyone sat in the sunshine around their table of house food, beautifully decorated with banners painted by the Lower Sixth. The house members also dressed up in their house colours, some perhaps going a little further in the task than others — two giant yellow bananas featured near the Haberdasher table!

Full up with the lovely food, we set about the rest of the busy afternoon. Mr Kum had erected a voice-over and music system under the tree, and he announced the activities as they came round, whilst a team of artistic Sixth Formers painted faces with anything from house colours and letters to butterflies and flowers. The afternoon kicked off with a very exciting tug-of-war between the highly competitive Upper Sixth house members, egged on by equally competitive younger house members. There was a treasure hunt around the School for the juniors, organised by Dr Ouldridge; and Miss Millar and Mrs Wood had organised a house country dancing competition in Bradley Hall. Meanwhile there was a series of traditional races on the track on Leebourne for all age groups. The idea was that a representative from each year would compete for their house in a relay. The races culminated in a rather hilarious teacher's assault course race.

Next was the event which many had been eagerly anticipating. Not for the faint hearted, 'Worm Charming' was the brain-child of Dr Rudling, and required the contestants from each house to 'charm' as many worms out of the soil in their quadrant as they could in a time limit. It involved acting a bit like a seagull — jumping up and down on the ground (apparently creating vibrations which the worms like, causing them to come to the surface), and mimicking rain with a bucket of soapy water. Unlikely though it sounds, the techniques worked and worm numbers reached about 40 in one square metre.

Finally there was a giant game of musical statues on the bottom tennis courts which involved the whole school. It took some time, but eventually, with expert judging from the Upper Sixth, we managed to find a winner out of the hundreds. It was a great end to a fantastic afternoon, which everyone enjoyed. The sun shone throughout, the food was lovely and the activities were well organised. It was a huge success and fabulous fun.

Becci Gosling (Upper Sixth; member of Head Girl Team 2007–2008)

For me, one of the best things about the picnic was the participation throughout the year groups, from oldest to youngest, all joining in. It was a marvellously fun afternoon, filled with happy, smiling girls, and that's what I'll remember most about the spirit of the Maynard when I look back in years to come.

Thanksgiving Service

Dolores Carbonari (Lower 3)

As it grew closer to the day of the service, I thought how lucky I was to be chosen to speak at the 350th celebration service at the Cathedral. Ever since I had been asked to write a speech and actually say it to an audience, I had been going over it again and again, painstakingly, until I was word-perfect.

The morning of the service I had butterflies the size of pelicans, fluttering about inside my stomach. It must have been a nightmare to be around me at school that day, and if you didn't know me, or what I was doing, you probably would have thought I was a raving idiot — murmuring the words every spare minute of the day and constantly pestering my friends, to listen to me practise, and asking if it was all right!

At approximately 12.30pm, I went for a practice at the Cathedral, with all the other speakers. I had many a polite chat, comparing the Maynard from 30 or 40 years ago to the present day with a very nice Old Maynardian. In practice it was encouraging to hear other people talk (and maybe falter slightly) which took the edge off the pressure. It also meant I got a sneak preview of what was going to happen at the service.

It was now the end of the morning preparations — this was it. All the rehearsing and practice was over, and now I had to show my hard work to, I think, approximately a thousand people!

Before the service, I walked down with my class and the rest of the School to the Cathedral. As we arrived and started to shuffle into the Cathedral in our groups, it all started to become real.

I went and sat down in my seat, and felt so proud and superior when I saw my name card, laminated, on a seat reserved for me on the front row!

Before it was my go, along with all the other two-minute-memory speakers, there was the actual service of prayers, readings and a few hymns. Then, the speeches — Doctor West and the past headmistress, Miss Murdin, along with the Bishop of Exeter whose sermon certainly set people thinking.

My time was getting closer as the first two-minute-memory speakers had said their speeches. And then, oh no, it was me. Those pelican-sized butterflies somehow managed to get even bigger! I felt quite woozy and faint with nerves. I got up almost wobbling as I walked and turned on the microphone; glancing quickly up, I saw a thousand or so beady eyes staring straight back at me expectantly — which didn't exactly help!

I said my speech and felt as though I had eaten a raw chilli! It always surprises me that when I perform or speak on stage I feel as though my face is burning, but people always say — like after the service — 'Were you nervous? 'Cos you looked as cool as a cucumber.' If only they knew!

I wobbled back to my seat and felt a huge sigh of relief as I realised it was over. Done. I just sat back and enjoyed the rest of the service.

It was lovely when it was finished and I went outside to be congratulated by hundreds of people and many of them I didn't even know! I enjoyed it so much, I will treasure that day forever. I would like to thank Mrs Reynolds for giving me the opportunity.

Katy Pearce (Lower Sixth; member of Head Girl Team 2008–2009)

The current Maynard community, as well as many old girls, filled Exeter Cathedral to celebrate 350 years of The Maynard School. The service included some Maynard memories, including one where a pupil, now in the Sixth Form, reminisced about her seven years at the Maynard. Hymns, sung by both the Chamber Choir and the congregation, filled the cathedral and readings were given. The service itself was led by The Reverend Dr Alexandra Clarke, a Maynard Old Girl herself. As the high-spirited congregation filed out onto Cathedral Green, many talking about celebrating 400 years of The Maynard, the bells were rung in honour of the occasion, and in anticipation of further celebration in the future. I was involved in showing the congregation to their seats – including the Lord Mayor of Exeter! I felt that the service was a fitting tribute to 350 years of the school, and a fantastic part of the celebrations.

Pam Wilson (1940–42; Head of Classics 1960–84; Deputy Head 1967–90)

The whole School and many Old Maynardians, parents and friends filled the Cathedral on 7th May for the Service, and the historic venue, the celebration of our heritage, the music, even the glorious weather, all contributed to make this a memorable day.

The themes of the Service were expressed in the hymns: 'Lord, for the years your love has kept and guided, we bring our thanks today', and 'Be thou my vision, O Lord of my heart'; and in the readings: 'Get wisdom, get insight', and 'There are many members, yet one body'. The Reverend Dr Alexandra Clarke (OM), led the prayers; Miss Murdin and Dr West read the Lessons; the Maynard Chamber Choir sang; and three current pupils and one Old Maynardian, giving brief impressions of their life in School, echoed my own memories from the 1940s: a happy community, with friendly people, encouraging a healthy spirit of enterprise, and a lively interest in learning.

This was the occasion to reflect on our past and present and hopes for the future, and I felt that the traditions and original ethos of the School have been preserved and continue, and deserve to be celebrated with thanksgiving.

Gala Concert

Emma Watkinson (Form 2N)

I was only there for the first half so I didn't see the Middle School Choir and other performances. Mr Horton's orchestra was brilliant and every now and again there were big BANGS that made you jump out of your skin! I thought Mr Crew's choir at the Service was awesome and I really enjoyed relaxing to the varied sounds. I really treasured singing in the first half because I could see that the audience were appreciating watching us, experiencing just the beginning of our school life, singing like never before. I would like to thank Mrs Austin for organising it and helping us learn the words. It was a great moment of my life that I will never forget.

Becci Gosling

The Gala Concert on 8th May was a special event for many Maynardians, old and new, and especially for those of us enjoying it as our last concert at the Maynard. The music was phenomenal, the setting was stunning and there was an excitement for audience and performers alike. During the first half, the Orchestra and Chamber Orchestra played both spirited and moving pieces and the soloists took our breath away with their talent and musicality. Even the junior department played their part and stood on the platform singing proudly with their neat Black Watch tartan pinafores and bright eyes a-shine. The second half was wonderfully varied, including performances by all ages and of all styles. The concert ended with current and old Maynardians singing the School Song as proudly as the juniors had sung earlier in the evening. For me, it was a spectacular concert to end my time at the Maynard, and the buzz of the Maynardian spirit celebrating our 350 years left me feeling proud to be part of it.

Pam Wilson

The Gala Concert, performed to a packed audience, was a lively event, notable for the large number of girls taking part and the inspiring music of the orchestras, jazz band, choirs and soloists. The programme was full of variety, and we all enjoyed the freshness of the performers who were confident and enthusiastic, and in no way daunted by the awe-inspiring place. The whole Junior Department sat on the platform motionless, and then sprang into life and entertained with two songs, the lyrics of *School is Cool!* being their own composition. A special treat was to hear two soloists, Hannah Dalton, clarinet, and Marie Langrishe, violin, who played with great skill and sensitivity. The evening ended with an impromptu gallop through the School Song, led by two Old Maynardians, who felt that the occasion demanded such a fitting conclusion.

Science Timeline

On 1st July, the Science department mounted a living timeline of the life and work of 76 scientists from the past 350 years, portrayed by the girls from Upper 3 to Lower 6. Working in groups of two to three, the girls had carried out independent research in their Science lessons during the previous week. Each group produced a display of its findings, including a poster and a short presentation. During the morning all the displays were arranged in timeline order and 10 sets of judges, including staff, former pupils and present-day scientists, were asked to judge the presentations and find a winning team in each year group, for a 'Science Communicators' award. As well as the more formal judging, everyone who visited was able to vote for their favourite scientist from the timeline. The Science department, which was abuzz with activity and passion for the various scientists, was visited by the whole school, including the Junior girls who were fascinated to see the work of their older peers.

Big Reunion Weekend and Ball

Over the weekend of 5th/6th July around 400 Old Maynardians came back to School for what was the biggest single gathering of former pupils ever. On the Saturday, there were six individual reunions for the leavers of 1955, 1956, 1957, 1968, 1973 and 1979 — a total of 150, followed, that evening, by a 350th Ball at Sandy Park attended by around 300 former pupils and teachers, current staff and parents. The next day another 250 or so Old Maynardians, ranging from a leaver of 1934, to the most recent of 2000, visited the School. As well as a special 'old girls' netball match, all the guests were treated to a fantastic buffet lunch prepared by the School chef and his team. They were able to tour the School buildings and grounds, to see what had changed and what they still recognised from their respective eras, and both days ended with everyone singing a rousing rendition of the two School songs followed by the School bell! It was a wonderful opportunity for Old Maynardians, who had travelled from all around the UK, and even across the world, to catch up with classmates they hadn't, in many cases, seen for decades. It was, without doubt, a fantastic event that will live long in the memory of all involved.

Summer Fete

With everyone already excited at the prospect of breaking up for the summer holidays the following day, the School became a hive of activity and strange happenings on 9th July, with the 350th Anniversary Summer Fête. As well as the usual tombola, 'name the teddy', cake, bottles and book stalls, we had Sumo wrestling in the Bradley Hall, fortune telling, a photo booth, maggot racing, juggling, hand bell ringing, and 'pin the sideburns on Elvis'! The MPA served wonderful Cream Teas in the Dining Centre and various girls provided busking entertainment during the afternoon. It was a wonderfully happy event and raised over £1,000 for the 350th Anniversary Appeal, for Nosiphiwo, a student in South Africa whom the Maynard is supporting, and for 'The Colour of Hope', a charity in Peru set up by Old Maynardian Amy New.

And as if all of that wasn't enough, at the time of this book going to press, preparations were underway for the special Musical Soirée at Ugbrooke House on 11th October; the long-awaited staff play, *Daisy Pulls It Off*, in the last week of November; and the Christmas Carol Service, which this year will be held in Exeter Cathedral on 18th December, the last day of term, to round off in style a truly amazing year in the Maynard School's long history.

A Few Notable Pupils

One of the earliest surviving school magazines records the memories of **Clara Andrews**, who was among the first High School pupils during the time of the first Head, Nora Hall (1877-1891). Miss Hall's school rules were severe, involving pupils not talking or making signs to each other during school hours. Clara remembers being called to see the Head after acknowledging that she had broken this rule. Clara wrote: 'She met me with her eyes full of tears, and said she had trusted me entirely. I explained that I was one of four voluntary workers in a German class, which prepared lessons alone in a classroom with only one set of books between us, and rather than commit the greater crime of speaking, we had made silent signs for the books we needed. I shall never forget the rapid transition from tearful severity to infectious laughter when she said, "Clara, dear, I think you must be allowed to speak in this case."' Clara went on to found the National Children's Adoption Society.

Three Maynardians from the 1880s and 1890s went on to practise medicine, and one of them, **Mary Townsend**, went on to run a hospital at Peshawar, now in Pakistan but then in India's North West Frontier, along with **Miss Brown**, a former member of staff, who left to change career for a degree in medicine, and founded the School of Medicine for Indian Women at Ludhiana in the Punjab. Although there was a Science laboratory at the school, by the 1920s prospective medical students from the Maynard were given supplementary science teaching in Zoology and Physics at the Royal Albert Memorial College (now the Phoenix Arts Centre), in the centre of the City.

During the First World War former pupils showed how intrepid they were. One, **Edith Rowe**, worked with her sister nursing behind the front lines at Abbeville in France, where she died of cerebral meningitis. Another, **Gertrude Bacon** ran reconnaissance balloon flights with her father to help the war effort.

Dame Irene Vanbrugh (1872-1949) and **Violet Vanbrugh** (1867-1942). Born Barnes (they later adopted the stage name of Vanbrugh), Irene and her sister Violet were pupils when their father was Vicar of Heavitree. They both became famous actresses, with distinguished, successful careers – something both unusual and notable for women at the time. Violet concentrated more on Shakespearean roles and Irene became the more high-profile actress, perhaps because she acted in some of the best and most controversial plays of the period – those of Oscar Wilde, George Bernard Shaw and Henrik Ibsen. In 1938 she celebrated her stage jubilee with a performance at His Majesty's Theatre in front of the Queen and Duchess of Kent, and was created a Dame Commander of the British Empire in 1941. She maintained contact with the school, revisiting in 1927 to open the school fête and writing a long article entitled 'Acting as a Profession', for the 1930/31 school magazine.

Mildred Veitch was a star pupil. In 1906, when she was in Upper 5, she was the school Tennis champion, won two separate school prizes for examination success, and was awarded Oxbridge Joint Board 'letters' for History, French and Maths. In 1909, she went to St Hilda's Oxford, and went on to become a History mistress, first at Queen Margaret School, Scarborough, then at Sydenham High School, before returning, in 1919, to join her father in the family firm of Robert Veitch & Son, Exeter, plantsmen with an international reputation. In 1929 she became head of the firm, moving it from New North Road to Alphington. In 1969, with her health failing and no other 'Veitch' available to continue the family business she sold it to St Bridget Nurseries. She died in Exmouth in 1971.

In 1984, the Mastermind winner for that year was Heavitree-born Old Maynardian **Miss Margaret Harris**, whose father, Mr Harris, was the School Caretaker. Margaret achieved the highest score ever recorded in the 11 years of the finals, her chosen subject being 'The life and work of Cecil Rhodes'. At the time of her win Margaret was Deputy Head of Woolston School in Southampton.

Professor Dame Margaret Turner Warwick (Harvey Moore) left the Maynard in 1942 for Lady Margaret Hall, Oxford, and went on to have an exceptionally distinguished medical career becoming, in 1989, the first woman President of the Royal College of Physicians. *Living Medicine*, her adult memoirs and reflections on medicine and other things was published in 2005.

Most Maynard girls from one family?

Amal Khreisheh 1995-2001 Lady Margaret Hall, Oxford (Classics) Graduate Trainee at Exeter & Plymouth Museums doing MA in Museum Studies

Nada Khreisheh 1996-2003 Exeter University (BA Archaeology) Now doing MA in Experimental Archaeology at Exeter

Yasmine Khreisheh 1998-2005 1st year Photography degree at Cambridge School of Arts

Suhaila Khreisheh 1999-2006 2nd year Arabic and Modern Middle Eastern Studies at Pembroke College, Oxford

Ameera Khreisheh 2003-(2010)

Reem Khreisheh 2005-(2012)

By 2012 Khreisheh sisters will have been at the Maynard continuously for 17 years!

Most Maynardian Maynardian?

We think that Annabel Hope, a current Sixth Former, may be the Maynardian with the earliest Maynardian connections. Adelaide Bayley, her fourth cousin via her mother (Lynda Bayley, now Lyn Hope, School Librarian), was born in 1872 and attended the Maynard towards the end of the 19th century. Although we don't know exactly when she was a pupil she is listed as an Old Maynardian in the very first issue of the school magazine in 1902. Adelaide became a professional singer, never married, and lived at 4 Powderham Crescent, an extremely wealthy and prestigious area of the city at that time. She died in 'Exeter City Hospital' in 1957.

The Maynard School ~ Key dates

Year	School Event
1602	Sir John Maynard is born.
1632	Elize Hele dies. Leaves fortune to be allocated by four trustees for 'godly and pious uses'.
1656	John Maynard and Elize Stert, Elize Hele's two surviving trustees, set up a charitable school for poor girls in Exeter.
1662	Maynard and Stert purchase the Great House in Mary Arches Street as separate school for Blue Maids. Pass responsibility to City Council.
1690	Sir John Maynard dies.
1862	Charity Commission recommends closure of school due to poor financial state. Endowment money reabsorbed by St John's Hospital Trust. The Great House is sold and demolished. Remaining few girls move to Larkbeare House.
1877	Money is reallocated for foundation of Maynard School for Girls. Miss Nora (Eleanora) Hall appointed Headmistress.
1878	Land for new school is purchased on Barnfield Estate.
1881	Finances are conveyed to commence building work.
1882	New school building completed and opened.
1883	School Hall is added.
1891	Miss Hall leaves; Miss Caroline Turner, already a member of staff, becomes Headmistress. Earliest School registers from this date.
1894	Cookery room and Science laboratory are added to school.
1900	School meal provision starts.
1901	Miss Turner leaves; Miss Florence Purdie becomes Headmistress. Summerlands is purchased as a boarding house.
1902	First issue of school magazine: Exeter High School Magazine. Inaugural meeting of revived Maynard School Old Girls' Society (MSOGS). School orchestra is formed.
1903	First School inspection.
1904	New Sports Pavilion is funded and established in new sports field in Matford Avenue. Open-flame gas burners are replaced by incandescent gas mantles (by Miss Purdie).
1905	Hot water radiators are extended from corridors into classrooms.
1907	New tennis court is completed. Gym apparatus installed in School Hall.
1908	Miss Purdie leaves; Miss Ethel Trenerry becomes Headmistress.

Year	School Event
1909	New Fives Court is completed.
1911	Name 'Maynard School' is formally adopted in place of Exeter High School for Girls. First School Sports Day held. Summerlands boarding house expands into adjoining house.
1912	Governors purchase Tregear, garden and tennis court (£3,350)
1913	Tregear alterations completed and boarders move in. Summerlands closes down temporarily. Extra boarders are accommodated in Headmistress's house in main school. Instead of Sports Day, summer fête is held to raise money for new asphalt tennis court.
1914	World War I is declared.
1918	World War I ends. School Girl Guides Company set up.
1919	Miss Trenerry leaves; Miss Clara Dixon becomes Headmistress. Summerlands re-opens as a boarding house.
1920	House system is started by Miss Dixon. School song is written by Miss Lily Parsons (Classics mistress and former Head Girl). Music composed by Miss Mary Alcock (new Music mistress). Petronella Snowball is first Head Girl to be recorded on Main Hall panelling.
1921	Amy Clogg, Head Girl, wins scholarship for Natural Sciences at Newnham College, Cambridge.
1923	Traceyville is purchased (£2,250).
1924	Electric lighting is installed throughout school, replacing gas lights. Junior School pupils move into Traceyville.
1925	Playing fields adjoining Traceyville are purchased for £750.
1933	Fund is started for new hard tennis court. New table and chair for stage in Hall is presented by MSOGS as memorial to Miss Hall.
1935	Miss Dixon retires due to ill-health; Miss Elsie May Ryan becomes Headmistress. Speech day is held at Barnfield Hall — first time not at School.
1937	Swimming lessons start, in King's Alley baths. First school trip abroad: Bayeux and Arromanches.
1938	New classrooms and hall are opened in Traceyville. Purdie Memorial Library is formally opened by Dean of Exeter. Air-raid shelter dug.
1939	First Sports Day since 1917 is held. World War II is declared.
1942	Summerlands is destroyed in blitz. Main school, Traceyville and Tregear all damaged. Tregear deeds and other records lost.
1945	World War II ends.
1949	Last year of Maynard boys in Kindergarten.
1951	O- and A-level examinations replace Lower and Higher School Certificates
1954	New Dining Centre opens.
1957	New Gymnasium is built.
1958	Gymnasium and new Biology laboratory officially opened. Tercentenary Celebrations.
1962	Miss Ryan retires; Miss Joan Bradley becomes Headmistress.
1963	Boarding ceases in Tregear, the last boarding house. Solid fuel boiler system is replaced by oil-fired system.

Year	School Event
1966	First Rennes exchange.
1968	Governors agree to Miss Bradley's proposal for building of new, dedicated Sixth Form block (Ryan House).
1970	Dedication service and official opening of Ryan House. Sixth Form no longer required to wear uniform. Speech day, in the University Great Hall, is held for the first time in the evening.
1972	Traceyville fire; building is badly damaged. First male member of staff appointed.
1974	First Hildesheim exchange (in conjunction with Exeter School).
1975	School becomes fully independent as Direct Grant system ends (in operation since 1922).
1979	Miss Bradley retires (December).
1980	Miss Felicity Murdin becomes Headmistress (January). First school ski-ing trip.
1981	MPA (Maynard Parents' Association) is formed. First event is a cheese and wine party.
1982	Centenary celebrations for the opening of the Main School building.
1983	New Biology laboratory is completed.
1984	Chairman of the Old Maynardians Society, Jeanne Shattock, is killed in the Brighton IRA bombing.
1985	New Sports Hall (Bradley Hall) opens.
1989	School magazine records first Open Evening.
1990	Foundation stone is laid for Pring Building (Science and Mathematics). Pring Building is completed and opened.
1991	First Old Boys' reunion; eight boys attend.
1996	Dedication of the Blue Boy statue on Maynard site.
1999	Miss Murdin retires (December).
2000	Dr Daphne West becomes Headmistress (January). Government's Assisted Places Scheme ceases.
2004	Refurbished Ryan House is opened by Miss Murdin. Pupil Emily Webster killed; other pupils and Dr West seriously injured in Ufton Nervet train crash.
2008	School celebrates its 350th anniversary. Murdin Link is opened by Miss Murdin. Dr West takes early retirement (December).
2009	Ms Bee Hughes becomes Headmistress (January).

List of subscribers

We are especially grateful to the following Old Maynardians and other friends of the School, who have supported this publication by subscribing for copies in advance.

Averil Anderson
Judith Attley
Jazmine and Sophie Bailey
May Baker
Mrs Thelma Baker (Hamon)
Sally Baldwin
Rosemary Baxter (Wall)
Izzi and Claudia Beresford
Sophie Biddell
Aurelia Tryphena Bishop
Blickling Hall
Kathleen Boreham (Born)
Dodie Bowman
Abby Bowman
Robyn Bowman
Mrs Shona Bradley (Ferguson)
Stephanie Bray (Wills)
Joy Brealey (Trethewey)
Catherine Brooks (Webber)
Rohanna Brown
Anna Bruce-Jones (Skinner)
Dr and Mrs Burgess
Sheila Burgess
Edith Burrow
Hilary Came
Sally Campbell (Sheppard)
Elizabeth Carne
Marjorie Carrington (Fairweather)
Rosemary Carrington (Harrison-Ainsworth)
Emanuela Cesaratto
Mrs Georgina Connor (Shilcock)
Pauline Cooper
Margaret Corbett-Winder
Penelope Cowman
Sheila M Cox
Alison Crawford (Beale)
Jean Davis
Madeleine (Pip) Davis
Fiona and Nancy Dawrant
Mary Ellis
Leila Ellis
Melanie Etherton
Susan Evans
Tammy Falloon (Flinn)
Tara and Sophie Folland
Elizabeth Gaisford
Aydan and Yasmin Gasimova
Dinah Gavanda
Sarah Gay (Chamberlain)
Melanie Gibbs
Heather Godwin-Rolfe (Blackmore)
Jenny Golding (McSkimming)
Marion Golmohammadi (Sercombe)
Sarah Gooding
Grace Goss-Custard
Samantha Grainger (Webber)
Mrs Morag Grammaticas (Ferguson)
Elizabeth Groves (Grantham)
Ellie Guest
Tessa Gullick
Liz Guppy (Thackray)
Margaret Guyver
P Jean Hall
Judith Hall (Roberts)
Jo Hallett (Hargreaves)
Pip and Issy Halpin
Margaret Ham (Fleming)
Helen Hammond (Savage)
Margaret Hampshire (Rae)
Beth Hannaford
Helen Harris (Warren)
Alexandra Hatherly
Val Hawkins (Herneman)
Dr Maggie Hayward (Long)
Jillian Hearn
The Hearth Family
Jocelyn Hemming (Fortescue-Foulkes)
Dr E P Henderson
Margaret Henshaw
Erika Herpoldt
Maggie Heywood
Patricia P Hignell (Nixon)
Catherine Hill (Savage)
Tara Hooper
Lyn Hope (Bayley)
Nick and Alison Horton
Dorothy Houghton (Ryan)
Gemma Hoult
Sarah Howard (Spencer)
Tom Hughes-Parry
Adele Humphreys (Cox)
The Humphries Family
Rachel Irvine
Catherine Anne Jackson
Charlotte Sarah Jackson
Eileen Jones
Mrs Audrey Jones (Etheridge)
Jane Jones (Patrick)
Tom Jump
Janet Kennedy
Bridget Kirby (Pearse)
Peggy Lancaster
Emma Laws
Pamela Le Bas (Dyer)
Georgina Legg (Pierce)
Valerie Livsey (Force)
Jayne Loats (Gorman)
Stephanie Lytton
Leo Mackenzie (Stapleton)
Danielle Magee
Jo Makin (Pickard)
Cristiana Merisi
Sally E Messenger (Wise)
Alexandra Milford
Deborah Miller
Helen Miller (Gentle)
Sarah Moffat
Catherine Moody
Phyl Mullins (Hodges)
Katherine Louise Mundy
Felicity Murdin
Mrs Clare Murley (Hodges)
Elizabeth Murphy (Hales)
Hetti Murray
Jennifer Naish (Thorn)
Alison Napier
Mrs Frances Nieduszynska (Oxford)
Gillian Norman (Newlands)
Angela Nott
Vivienne M Owen
Jane Page (Lane)
Rosemary Parsons (Ponsford)
Ursula Perry
Anne Pidsley (Wheaton)
Joanna Portman
Ian Powell
Katherine Ralph (Janes)
Liz Ratcliffe (Wenham)
Pat Read
Janet Regan
Helen Reynolds
Kate, Philly and Harriet Reynolds
Anne Rhodes (Barrett)
Helen Richardson
Geoffrey and Janet Robb
Elizabeth Rogers (Hatch)
Claire and Olivia Rowe
Anne Sargent (Edwards)
Sarah Sayers (Davies)
Annette Seale
Alison Selley
Lisa Sensier (Clarke)
Alison Shannon (Donne)
Donna Sharp
N and B Shiel
Dr Jean M Shields (Philip)
Marilyn Skinner (Fulford)
Daphne Smith
Janice Smith
Rosemary Sookias (Axe)
Abbey and Pippa Southall
Samantha Spriggs (Ernest)
Barbara Inge, formerly Stagg (Townson)
Cynthia Staines (Shankland-Smith)
Roberta Stather (Williams)
Jill Stephens (Clark)
Mrs Frances Stephens (Martin)
A Ruth Stone
Hilary Stookes
Bena Stuart
Lynn Stuckey
Mrs Diana Swayne (Goodchild)
Brenda Taylor
Jenny Taylor (Mayhead)
Mrs Jutta Tew
Miss Camilla Tew
Polly Thompson
Michelle Thompson (Reed)
Shaenna Tough (Stephens)
Dr Elizabeth Toy
Cathy Trotter
Marjorie Trusted
Margaret Tudeau Clayton
Anna K Turner
Sophie M Turner
Rachel Turner
Geraldine Turner (Purchase)
Germana Viviani
G Waddams (Whitfield)
Rosie Walker
Jordan Walker
Catrina Walters (Marsh)
Mrs Jane Waterfall (Tolchard)
Mary Way (Stark)
Lisa Weekes (Maynard)
Mary Whitear
Sylvia Wickenden
Rosemary Wilkinson (Burdett)
Miss Chloë Wood
Daphne Worraker (Wippell)
Georgia Zervudachi

Index

Cover images

Front cover, top: Main School, c1990; bottom: Drill in School Hall, c1920

Back cover:

<table>
<tr><td>House badge:
Goldsmiths</td><td>Miss Nora Hall
Head
1877–1891</td><td>House badge:
Armourers</td><td>Miss Caroline
Turner
Head
1891–1901</td><td>Lower Sixth,
1963</td></tr>
<tr><td>Sir John
Maynard
1602–1690</td><td>Old school
blazer badge</td><td>Dr Daphne
West
Head
2000–2008</td><td>Old school logo,
still used by Old
Maynardians
Society</td><td>Miss Elsie May
Ryan
Head
1935–1962</td></tr>
<tr><td>Miss Felicity
Murdin
Head
1980–1999</td><td>House badge:
Merchant
Venturers</td><td>Miss Clara
Dixon
Head
1919–1935</td><td rowspan="2">Blue Boy
Statue
situated
outside
Pring
building</td><td>350th Logo</td></tr>
<tr><td colspan="2" rowspan="2">Tregear</td><td>Miss Joan
Bradley
Head
1962–1979</td><td>Miss Florence
Purdie
Head
1901–1908</td></tr>
<tr><td>New school logo
adopted in 1997</td><td>Ms Bee Hughes
Head from
January 2009</td><td>House badge:
Haberdashers</td></tr>
</table>

N.B. Sadly, we have been unable to locate an image of Miss Ethel Trenerry, Head 1908–1919.